Medicinal plants with anti-ageing potential and evaluation protocols

A comprehensive guide on medicinal plants having anti-ageing and anti-wrinkle potential, *in-vitro* evaluation protocols including a case study. Useful for research scholars, practitioners of alternative medicines and students

Chanchal Garg, PhD

(Main Author)

TABLE OF CONTENTS

Contributors

Chanchal Garg, PhD Post Doctoral Research Fellow (UGC-PDFW)
Department of Pharmaceutical Sciences,
Maharshi Dayanand University,
Rohtak, haryana, India

Munish Garg, PhD Professor,
Department of Pharmaceutical Sciences,
Maharshi Dayanand University,
Rohtak, haryana, India

Harpal S Buttar, PhD Professor,
Department of Pathology & Laboratory Medicine,
University of Ottawa,
Faculty of Medicine, Ottawa,
Ontario, Canada.

Vaibhav Walia, PhD Assistant Professor
Faculty of Pharmacy
DIT University,
Dehradun, India

Sukender Kumar Research Scholar,
Department of Pharmaceutical Sciences,
Maharshi Dayanand University,
Rohtak, haryana, India

Amit Kumar Research Student (Passed out)
Department of Pharmaceutical Sciences,
Maharshi Dayanand University,
Rohtak, haryana, India

Anti-ageing Medicinal Plants

Chanchal Garg, Sukender Kumar, Munish Garg

In this chapter, the recent studies mostly relevant with anti-ageing activity of plant species along with their pharmacological effects against molecular processes driving skin ageing, are summarized. The research articles, published since 2010 to 2020, were selected from Pubmed and Science direct using relevant keywords including anti-ageing potential of medicinal plants, anti-ageing medicinal plants and anti-ageing activity of medicinal plants.

Table: 1. Anti-ageing activity of medicinal plants

S No	Species and family	Plant part	Pharmacological activity	Reference
1.	*Clerodendrum glabrum* E.(Verbenaceae)	Root, stems, fruit, bark	Inhibition of hyaluronidase, collagenase and elastase, antioxidant activity	1
2.	*Peltophorum africanum* Sond.(Fabaceae)	Leaves, seeds, bark, stem	Inhibitory effects on hyaluronidase, collagenase and elastase, antioxidant activity	1
3.	*Psychotria capensis* (Eckl.)(Rubiaceae)	Root, stems, Leaves, seeds,	Inhibition of enzymes hyaluronidase, collagenase and elastase, antioxidant activity	1
4.	*Schotia brachypetala* Sond.	Bark, leaves	Inhibition of hyaluronidase,	1

	(Fabaceae)		collagenase and elastase, antioxidant activity	
5.	*Zingiber officinale* Roscoe (Zingiberaceae)	Rhizomes	Diminish oxidative stress and pro-inflammatory cytokines	2
6.	*Glycyrrhiza glabra*(Fabaceae)	Root	Diminish oxidative stress and pro-inflammatory cytokines	2
7.	*Rosmarinus officinalis* L. (Labiatae)	Aerial parts	Diminish oxidative stress and pro-inflammatory cytokines	2
8.	*Peganum harmala* L. (Nitrariaceae)	Seed	Diminish oxidative stress and pro-inflammatory cytokines	2
9.	*Aloe vera* (Liliaceace)	Gel	Diminish oxidative stress and pro-inflammatory cytokines	2
10.	*Satureja hortensis* L. (Labiatae)	Aerial parts	Diminish oxidative stress and pro-inflammatory cytokines	2
11.	*Teucrium scordium* L.(Labiatae)	Aerial parts	Diminish oxidative stress and pro-inflammatory cytokines	2
12.	*Hypericum perforatum* L. (Hypericaceae)	Aerial parts	Diminish oxidative stress and pro-inflammatory cytokines	2
13.	*Silybum marianum* (L.) Gaertn. (Asteraceae)	Seed	Diminish oxidative stress and pro-inflammatory cytokines, anti-elastase effect	2,8
14.	*Elaeis guineensis* Jacq.	Leaves	Antioxidant activity	3

	(Palmaceae)			
15.	*Polygonum multiflorum* Thunb. (Polygonaceae)	Root	Stimulates growth hormone secretion via activation of the ghrelin receptor	4
16.	*Stereospermum suaveolens* (Roxb.) DC (Bignoniaceae)	Aerial parts	Attenuates intracellular ROS and stress (oxidative and thermal) level	5
17.	*Schisandra chinensis* (Turcz.) Baill (Schisandraceae)	Fruit	Nrf2-mediated HO-1 induction	6
18.	*Salvia officinalis* (Lamiaceae)	Leaves	Antioxidant and enzyme inhibitory activity, protective sunscreen against UV radiation.	7
19.	*Phyllanthus emblica* L. (Euphorbiaceae)	Fruit	Antioxidant property with moderate anti-collagenase activity.	8
20.	*Manilkara zapota* L.P. Royen (Sapotaceae)	Fruit	Inhibition of collagenase and elastase high but with moderate antioxidant effect	8
21.	*Curcurma longa* (Zingiberaceae)	Fresh leaves	Antioxidant and enzyme inhibitory activity	9
22.	*Oenanthe javanica* (Apiaceae)	Fresh leaves	Antioxidant and enzyme inhibitory activity	9
23.	*Vitex negundo* L. (Verbenaceae)	Fresh leaves	Antioxidant and enzyme inhibitory activity	9
24.	*Pluchea indica* (Asteraceae)	Fresh leaves	Antioxidant and enzyme inhibitory activity	9

25.	*Cosmos caudatus* (Asteraceae)	Fresh leaves	Antioxidant and enzyme inhibitory activity	9
26.	*Persicaria minus* (Polygonaceae)	Fresh leaves	Antioxidant and enzyme inhibitory activity	9
27.	*Aegle marmelos* L. (Rutaceae)	Unripe and ripe fruit pulp	Anti-elastase and antioxidant activity	10
28.	*Nyctanthes arbor-tristis* L. (Oleaceae)	Leaves	Anti-elastase and antioxidant activity	10
29.	*Musa paradisiaca* L. (Musaceae)	Terminal meristem of flower	Anti-elastase and antioxidant activity	10
30.	*Malaxis acuminata* D. (Orchidaceae)	Capsules	Antioxidant and enzyme inhibitory activity, high sun protection factor	11
31.	*Tagetes erecta* L. (Asteraceae)	Flower	Antioxidant activity	12
32.	*Onosma bracteatum* Wall (Boraginaceae)	Whole plant	Not reported	13
33.	*Boerhaavia diffusa* L. (Nyctaginaceae)	Root	Diminution of free radicals	14
34.	*Abies sibirica* (Penaceae)	Capsule	Induced genes of stress response, apoptosis regulation and tissue regeneration.	15
35.	*Asparagus racemosus* (Liliaceae)	Root	Antioxidant activity and promotes longevity	16
36.	*Acacia nilotica* (Leguminosae)	Leaves	Free radical scavenging activity	17, 25
37.	*Arctium lappa* (Asteraceae)	Seeds, Roots and Leaves	Strong free radical scavenger	18, 23
38.	*Premna integrifolia* Linn.	Stem bark	Reduce reactive oxygen species	19,24

			(ROS) levels and fat accumulation	
39.	*Aesculus hippocastanum* L. (Sapindaceae)	Seed	Antioxidative potential	20
40.	*Limonia acidissima* L. (Rutaceae)	Fruit	Antioxidant activity	21
41.	*Picea mariana*(Pinaceae)	Bark	Antioxidant and anti-enzymatic properties	22
42.	*Pinus banksania* (Pinaceae)	Bark	Antioxidant and anti-enzymatic properties	22
43.	*Betula alleghaniensis* (Betulaceae)	Bark	Antioxidant and anti-enzymatic properties	22
44.	*Acer rubrum* (Sapindaceae)	Bark	Antioxidant and anti-enzymatic properties	22
45.	*Ocimum basilicum* L. (Lamiaceae)	Stem bark	Antioxidant activity	24
46.	*Stereospermum suaveolens* (Bignoniaceae)	Aerial part	Control the oxidative and thermal stress, Enhance antioxidant enzyme levels by reducing cellular ROS levels	26
47.	*Bellis perennis* (Asteraceae)	Flowers	Promote collagen synthesis in normal human dermal fibroblasts (NHDFs)	27
48.	*Panax ginseng*(Araliaceae)	Root	Regulate collagen metabolism by procollagen type 1 and MMP-1expression in NHDFs, inhibit wrinkle formation and increase	28

			moisture in skin	
49.	*Crataegus pinnatifida*(Rosaceae)	Fruit	Regulate collagen metabolism by procollagen type 1 and MMP-1 expression in NHDFs, inhibit wrinkle formation and increase moisture in skin	28
50.	*Melilotus officinalis* (L.) Pall. (Fabaceae)	Flower	Collagen production, Stimulate skin cells and tissue regeneration	29
51.	*Lespedeza capitate* Michx.(Fabaceae)	Branches	Collagenase inhibition, Stimulate skin cells and tissue regeneration	29
52.	*Foeniculum vulgare* Mill. (Umbelliferae)	Seed	Free radical scavenging activity	30
53.	*Hypericum androsaemum* L. (Hypericaceae)	Red berries	Collagenase inhibitor	31
54.	*Juniperus communis* L. (Cupressaceae)	Berry essential oil	ROS detoxification, enhance stress resistance and reduces lipofuscin in *C. elegans*	32
55.	*Alkanna tinctoria* L. (Boraginaceae)	Root bark	Antioxidant, anti-elastase enzyme and sun protection activities	33
56.	*Panax ginseng* (Araliaceae)	Leaves	Reducetyrosinase activity,melanin content, mRNA expression of melanogenesis-	34

			associated transcription factor and tyrosinase in B16 cells	
57.	*Curcuma heyneana* Valeton & Zipj (Zingiberaceae)	Rhizome	Antioxidant, tyrosinase and collagenase inhibitor activity	35
58.	*Juglans regia* L. (Juglandaceae)	Male flower	Absorb UV, moderates inflammatory signallingand free radical scavenging capability.	36
59.	*Crinum latifolium* L. (Amaryllidaceae)	Fresh bulbs	Radical scavenging activity	37
60.	*Lycium barbarum* (Solanaceae)	Fruit	Free radical scavenging activity	38
61.	*Harungana madagascariensis* Lam.(Hypericaceae)	Aerial parts	Highly inhibitory to oxidants and to enzymes tyrosinase and elastase	39
62.	*Psorospermum aurantiacum* Engl. (Guttiferae)	Aerial part	Inhibit activity of oxidants and enzymes tyrosinase and elastase strongly	39

References

1. Ndlovu G, Fouche G, Tselanyane M, et al. *In vitro* determination of the anti-ageing potential of four southern African medicinal plants. *BMC Complement Altern Med.* 2013;13:304. https://doi.org/10.1186/1472-6882-13-304

2. Mohammadirad A, Aghamohammadali-Sarraf F, Badiei S, et al. Anti-ageing effects of some selected Iranian folk medicinal herbs-biochemical evidences. *Iran J Basic Med Sci.* 2013;16(11):1170-1180.

3. Soundararajan V., Sreenivasan S. Antioxidant activity of *Elaeis guineensis* leaf extract: An alternative nutraceutical approach in impeding ageing. APCBEE Procedia. 2012;2:153–159. doi: 10.1016/j.apcbee.2012.06.028.

4. Lo YH, Chen YJ, Chung TY, et al. Emoghrelin, a unique emodin derivative in Heshouwu, stimulates growth hormone secretion via activation of the ghrelin receptor. *J Ethnopharmacol.* 2015;159:1-8. doi:10.1016/j.jep.2014.10.063

5. Pant A, Asthana J, Yadav AK, et al. Verminoside mediates life span extension and alleviates stress in *Caenorhabditis elegans. Free Radic Res.* 2015;49(11):1384-1392. doi:10.3109/10715762.2015.1075017

6. Kang JS, Han MH, Kim GY, et al. Nrf2-mediated HO-1 induction contributes to antioxidant capacity of a *Schisandrae Fructus* ethanol extract in C2C12 myoblasts. *Nutrients.* 2014;6(12):5667-5678. doi:10.3390/nu6125667

7. Khare R, Upmanyu N, Jha M. Exploring the potential effect of Methanolic extract of *Salvia officinalis* against UV exposed skin ageing: *In vivo* and *in vitro* model [published online

ahead of print, 2019 Aug 8]. *Curr Ageing Sci.*2019;10.2174/1874609812666190808140549. doi:10.2174/1874609812666190808140549

8. Pientaweeratch S, Panapisal V, Tansirikongkol A. Antioxidant, anti-collagenase and anti-elastase activities of *Phyllanthus emblica, Manilkara zapota* and silymarin: an in vitro comparative study for anti-ageing applications. *Pharm Biol.* 2016;54(9):1865-1872. doi:10.3109/13880209.2015.1133658

9. Hussin M, Abdul Hamid A, Abas F, et al. NMR-Based Metabolomics Profiling for Radical Scavenging and Anti-Ageing Properties of Selected Herbs. *Molecules.* 2019;24(17):3208. Published 2019 Sep 3. doi:10.3390/molecules24173208

10. Kalyana Sundaram I, Sarangi DD, Sundararajan V, George S, Sheik Mohideen S. Poly herbal formulation with anti-elastase and anti-oxidant properties for skin anti-ageing. *BMC Complement Altern Med.* 2018;18(1):33. Published 2018 Jan 29. doi:10.1186/s12906-018-2097-9

11. Bose B, Choudhury H, Tandon P, Kumaria S. Studies on secondary metabolite profiling, anti-inflammatory potential, in vitro photoprotective and skin-ageing related enzyme inhibitory activities of Malaxis acuminata, a threatened orchid of nutraceutical importance. *J Photochem Photobiol B.* 2017;173:686-695. doi:10.1016/j.jphotobiol.2017.07.010

12. Moliner C, Barros L, Dias MI, et al. Edible Flowers of *Tagetes erecta* L. as Functional Ingredients: Phenolic Composition, Antioxidant and Protective Effects on *Caenorhabditis elegans.*

Nutrients. 2018;10(12):2002. Published 2018 Dec 18. doi:10.3390/nu10122002

13. Farooq U, Pan Y, Disasa D, Qi J. Novel Anti-Ageing Benzoquinone Derivatives from *Onosma bracteatum* Wall. *Molecules*. 2019;24(7):1428. Published 2019 Apr 11. doi:10.3390/molecules24071428

14. Rathor L, Pandey R. Age-induced diminution of free radicals by Boeravinone B in *Caenorhabditis elegans.Exp Gerontol.* 2018;111:94-106. doi:10.1016/j.exger.2018.07.005

15. Kudryavtseva A, Krasnov G, Lipatova A, et al. Effects of *Abies sibirica* terpenes on cancer- and ageing-associated pathways in human cells. *Oncotarget*. 2016;7(50):83744-83754. doi:10.18632/oncotarget.13467

16. Smita SS, Raj Sammi S, Laxman TS, Bhatta RS, Pandey R. Shatavarin IV elicits lifespan extension and alleviates Parkinsonism in *Caenorhabditis elegans*. *Free Radic Res.* 2017;51(11-12):954-969.
doi:10.1080/10715762.2017.1395419

17. Kalaivani T, Mathew L. Free radical scavenging activity from leaves of *Acacia nilotica* (L.) Wild. ex Delile, an Indian medicinal tree. *Food Chem Toxicol*. 2010;48(1):298-305. doi:10.1016/j.fct.2009.10.013

18. Ferracane R, Graziani G, Gallo M, Fogliano V, Ritieni A. Metabolic profile of the bioactive compounds of burdock (*Arctium lappa*) seeds, roots and leaves. *J Pharm Biomed Anal*. 2010;51(2):399-404. doi:10.1016/j.jpba.2009.03.018

19. Shukla V, Yadav D, Phulara SC, Gupta MM, Saikia SK, Pandey R. Longevity-promoting effects of 4-hydroxy-E-

globularinin in *Caenorhabditis elegans*. *Free Radic Biol Med.* 2012;53(10):1848-1856.

doi:10.1016/j.freeradbiomed.2012.08.594

20. Felipe MBMC, de Carvalho FM, Félix-Silva J, Fernandes-Pedrosa MF, Scortecci KC, Agnez-Lima LF, Batistuzzo de Medeiros SR. Evaluation of genotoxic and antioxidant activity of an *Aesculus hippocastanum* L. (Sapindaceae) phytotherapeutic agent. *Biomedicine&PreventiveNutrition.* 2013;3:261–266. https://doi.org/10.1016/j.bionut.2012.10.014

21. Darsini DTP, Maheshu V, Vishnupriya M, Nishaa S, Sasikumar JM. Antioxidant potential and amino acid analysis of underutilized tropical fruit *Limonia acidissima* L.*Free Radicals and Antioxidants.*2013;3:S62-S69. https://doi.org/10.1016/j.fra.2013.08.001

22. Royer M, Prado M, Garcia-Perez ME, Diouf PN, Stevanovic T. Study of nutraceutical, nutricosmetics and cosmeceutical potentials of polyphenolic bark extracts from Canadian forest species, *Pharma Nutrition.* 2013;1(4):158-167. http://dx.doi.org/10.1016/j.phanu.2013.05.001

23. Su S, Wink M. Natural lignans from *Arctium lappa* as anti-ageing agents in *Caenorhabditis elegans.Phytochemistry.* 2015;117:340-350. doi:10.1016/j.phytochem.2015.06.021

24. Asthana J, Pant A, Yadav D, Lal RK, Gupta M, Pandey R. *Ocimum basilicum* (L.)and *Premna integrifolia* (L.) modulate stress response and lifespan in *Caenorhabditis elegans. Industrial Crops and Products.*2015;76:1086–1093.

25. Sadiq MB, Tharaphan P, Chotivanich K, Tarning J, Anal AK. In vitro antioxidant and antimalarial activities of leaves, pods

and bark extracts of *Acacia nilotica* (L.) Del. *BMC Complement Altern Med*. 2017;17(1):372. Published 2017 Jul 18. doi:10.1186/s12906-017-1878-x

26. Asthana J, Yadav AK, Pant A, Pandey S, Gupta MM, Pandey R. Specioside ameliorates oxidative stress and promotes longevity in *Caenorhabditis elegans*. *Comp Biochem Physiol C Toxicol Pharmacol*. 2015;169:25-34. doi:10.1016/j.cbpc.2015.01.002

27. Morikawa T, Ninomiya K, Takamori Y, et al. Oleanane-type triterpene saponins with collagen synthesis-promoting activity from the flowers of Bellis perennis. *Phytochemistry*. 2015;116:203-212. doi:10.1016/j.phytochem.2015.05.011

28. Hwang E, Park SY, Yin CS, Kim HT, Kim YM, Yi TH. Anti-ageing effects of the mixture of *Panax ginseng* and *Crataegus pinnatifida* in human dermal fibroblasts and healthy human skin. *J Ginseng Res*. 2017;41(1):69-77. doi:10.1016/j.jgr.2016.01.001

29. Pastorino G, Marchetti C, Borghesi B, Cornara L, Ribulla S, Burlando B. Biological activities of the legume crops *Melilotus officinalis* and *Lespedeza capitata* for skin care and pharmaceutical applications. *Industrial Crops and Products* 2017;96:158–164.

30. Abdellaoui M, Bouhlali E dine T, Kasrati A, El Rhaffari L. The effect of domestication on seed yield, essential oil yield and antioxidant activities of fennel seed (*Foeniculum vulgare* Mill) grown in Moroccan oasis. *Journal of the Association of Arab Universities for Basic and Applied Sciences.*

2017;24(1):107–114.
https://doi.org/10.1016/j.jaubas.2017.06.005

31. Antognoni F, Lianza M, Poli F, et al. Polar extracts from the berry-like fruits of *Hypericum androsaemum* L. as a promising ingredient in skin care formulations. *J Ethnopharmacol.* 2017;195:255-265. doi:10.1016/j.jep.2016.11.029

32. Pandey S, Tiwari S, Kumar A, Niranjan A, Chand J, Lehri A, Chauhan PS. Antioxidant and anti-ageing potential of Juniper berry (*Juniperus communis* L.) essential oil in *Caenorhabditis elegans* model system. *Industrial Crops and Products.*2018;120:113–122.https://doi.org/10.1016/j.indcrop.2018.04.066

33. Jaradat NA, Zaid AN, Hussen F, Issa L, Altamimi M, Fuqaha B, Nawahda A, Assadi M, Phytoconstituents, antioxidant, sun protection and skin anti-wrinkles effects using four solvents fractions of the root bark of the traditional plant *Alkanna tinctoria* (L.). *European Journal of Integrative Medicine.* 2018;21:88-93. https://doi.org/10.1016/j.eujim.2018.07.003

34. Jiménez-Pérez ZE, Singh P, Kim YJ, et al. Applications of *Panax ginseng* leaves-mediated gold nanoparticles in cosmetics relation to antioxidant, moisture retention, and whitening effect on B16BL6 cells. *J Ginseng Res.* 2018;42(3):327-333. doi:10.1016/j.jgr.2017.04.003

35. Kusumawati I, Kurniawan KO, Rullyansyah S, et al. Anti-ageing properties of *Curcuma heyneana* Valeton & Zipj: A scientific approach to its use in Javanese tradition. *J Ethnopharmacol.* 2018;225:64-70. doi:10.1016/j.jep.2018.06.038

36. Muzaffer U, Paul VI, Prasad NR, Karthikeyan R, Agilan B. Protective effect of Juglans regia L. against ultraviolet B radiation induced inflammatory responses in human epidermal keratinocytes. *Phytomedicine.* 2018;42:100-111. doi:10.1016/j.phymed.2018.03.024

37. Chen MX, Huo JM, Hu J, Xu ZP, Zhang X. Amaryllidaceae alkaloids from *Crinum latifolium* with cytotoxic, antimicrobial, antioxidant, and anti-inflammatory activities. *Fitoterapia.* 2018;130:48-53. doi:10.1016/j.fitote.2018.08.003

38. Wang SF, Liu X, Ding MY, et al. 2-O-β-d-glucopyranosyl-ᴌ-ascorbic acid, a novel vitamin C derivative from *Lycium barbarum*, prevents oxidative stress. *Redox Biol.* 2019;24:101173. doi:10.1016/j.redox.2019.101173

39. Jacqueline NM, Frederic NN, Apeksha J, et al. The anti-ageing potential of medicinal plants in Cameroon - *Harungana madagascariensis Lam.* and *Psorospermum aurantiacum* Engl. prevent in vitro ultraviolet B light-induced skin damage. *European Journal of Integrative Medicine.* 2019;29:100925. doi:10.1016/j.eujim.2019.05.011

Mechanistic approaches in the selection of in-vitro methods for the evaluation of skin care products

**Chanchal Garg, Vaibhav Walia, Sukender Kumar,
Harpal S. Buttar, Munish Garg**

Abstract

Skin ageing is a physical and biochemical change characterized by the wrinkles, sagging skin, uneven tone, spots, discoloration, dull skin, loss of tensile strength, dehydration and formation of senescent cells. The underlying cause of skin ageing is the generation of reactive oxygen species (ROS) which results in the development of oxidative stress. Oxidative stress further results in the damage to the various components of skin including lipids, proteins, carbohydrates and DNA. ROS modulates various signal pathways like mitogen-activated protein kinase (MAPK), the Janus kinase (JAK), the nuclear factor – kappa B (NF-κB)/p65, the nuclear factor erythroid 2-related factor 2 (Nrf2) and signal transduction and activation of transcription (STST) which results in the genesis of the key characteristics of skin ageing. Several *in- vivo* and *ex-vivo* methods are available for the evaluation of skin care products but due to increased ethical interests, alternate methods like *in-vitro* test models are being preferred these days. These models are less time consuming and minimize the need for experienced laboratory personnel for handling the animals. In the present review, various *in-vitro* methods of analysis and the rationale of conduction of these assays for the evaluation of skin care formulations and products are being explored.

Keywords: Photoageing; *In-vitro* models; Skin care products; Ultraviolet radiation; Molecular mechanisms

Introduction

Skin is the largest and fastest-growing organ that covers the entire external surface of the body. It has three component layers, the epidermis (outermost layer), the dermis (beneath epidermis), and the hypodermis (deeper subcutaneous tissue), which differ significantly in their anatomy and function. The skin provides protection against the external environment, supports in regulation of body temperature, fluid balance, and give some protection against sunlight.[1-4] The collagen and elastin fibers present in the dermal tissue of the skin is modified or damaged due to external and internal causes which lead to wrinkles formation and sagging. The enhancement in the expression of MMP's (Matrix Metalloproteinases) produces the repetitive breakdown of collagen fibers which is responsible for the structural defect in the dermis leading to wrinkle development.[5] Skin ageing appears as a physical and biochemical change in the skin which includes wrinkles, sagging skin, uneven tone, spots, discoloration, dull skin, loss of tensile strength, dehydrated skin, and formation of senescent or ageing cells. The reduced skin elasticity is one of the primary causes of the skin ageing.[6]The main underlying cause of skin ageing is the generation of reactive oxygen species which results in oxidative stress, and due to the presence of excessive lipids, proteins, carbohydrates and DNA in the skin, it is the most affected part.[7,8]Though, the skin has its own natural defence mechanism to fight against the oxidative stress through the antioxidant enzymes like peroxidases, catalases and glutathione present in it but, the protection offered is rudimentary owing to the unrestricted productivity of reactive oxygen species (ROS). Besides ROS, increase exposure to the ultraviolet (UV) radiations also results in the skin damage characterized by the hyperpigmentation. However the continuous and excessive exposure to UV radiations may leads to the development of conditions like cutaneous squamous cell carcinoma, malignant melanoma, basal cell carcinoma of the skin and photoageing, which causes loss of skin tightness and the development of solar keratoses.[9,10]The studies have shown that the exposure of UV radiations remodel the extracellular matrix (ECM) by increasing the matrix metalloproteinases and reduce structural collagen and elastin.[11,12] There are various methods employed for evaluating the anti-ageing and antiwrinkle potential of skin care products and formulations and assessing the skin ageing parameters. These include *in-vivo*, *ex-vivo* as well as *in-vitro* methods. In the present manuscript authors describe the skin components, skin ageing, oxidative damage to skin and the various methods for the evaluation in detail.

Skin components

Collagen is a fibrous protein present in the ECM and responsible for the tensile strength of skin.[13] Specifically, type I collagen is more abundant in the connective tissue. Collagen is mainly synthesized by the fibroblast cells present in the dermis and is degraded by the enzymes matrix metalloproteinases (MMPs) secreted by the epidermal keratinocytes and dermal fibroblasts.[14-17] MMP -1 degrades collagen into fragments which are further hydrolyzed by gelatinases (MMP-2 and MMP-9) resulting in the impairment of functions of dermis (figure 1). [18-21]

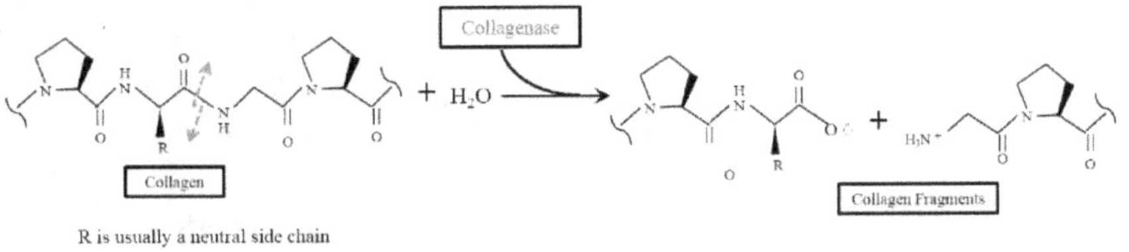

Figure 1: Degradation of collagen by Collagenase/MMP-1

The human skin colour is predominantly dependent on the presence of the pigment melanin.[24] This pigment is produced in the stratum basal layer of the skin epidermis by the melanocytes and plays a key role in preventing the skin from UV-induced damage.[25,26] Namely two types of melanin (figure 2) are produced in human skin: Eumelanins and Pheomelanins.[27]Tyrosinase is an essential enzyme responsible for the synthesis of melanin in melanocytes. It is also known as polyphenol oxidase (PPO). [22] Tyrosinase catalyses two major rate-limiting steps involved in the biosynthesis of melanin, i.e. tyrosine hydroxylation and oxidation of o-diphenyl product, L-DOPA (figure 3). L-DOPA on further oxidation yields a very reactive intermediate which on going through radical-coupling pathway further oxidizes to melanin.[23] Oxidation of tyrosine or phenylalanine by phenol oxidases results in the formation of o-dihydroxyphenylalanine (DOPA) and dopaquinone which further undergo cyclization in the presence of TYRP- 1 and TYRP-2 (tyrosinase related protein-1 and 2) to form 5,6-dihydroxyindole-2-carboxylic acid (DHICA) or 5,6-dihydroxyindole (DHI) to form Eumelanins (black or brown).[28,29]

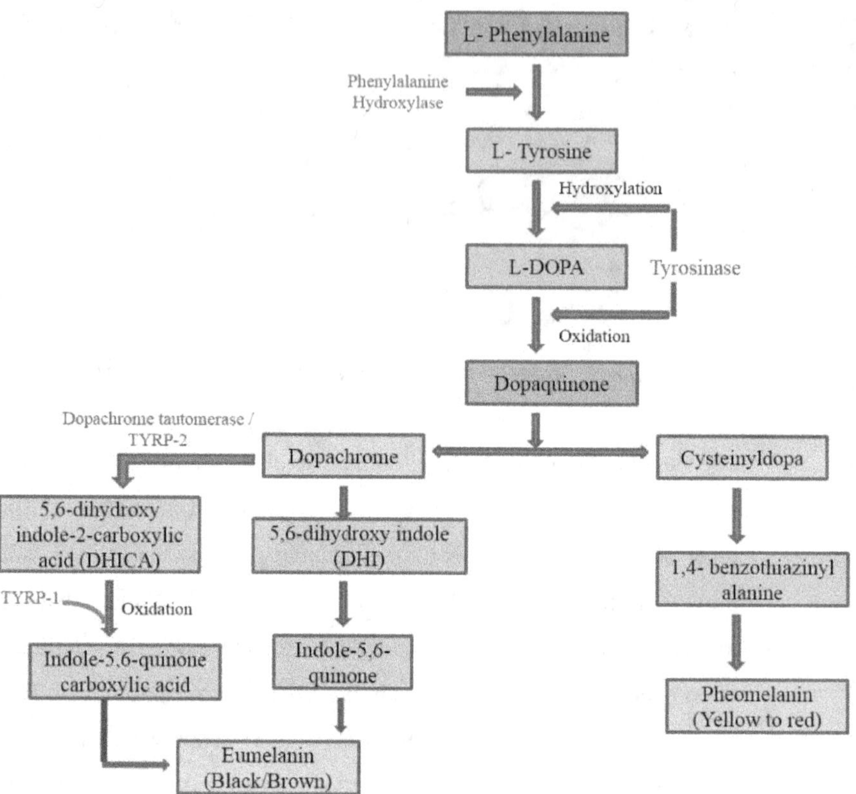

Figure 2: Production of dopachrome and melanin in melanocytes

Hyaluronic acid (HA) is a glycosaminoglycan (GAG) which retains water, present in the extracellular matrix (ECM) and keeps the body lubricated, moist and smooth. [30] It is primarily produced by mesenchymal cells along with some other types of cells also.[31-36] Hyaluronidases degrade HA by hydrolyzing a hexosaminidic β (1-4) linkage between D- glucuronic acid residues and N-acetyl-D-glucosamine (figure 3).[37-39] The degradation of hyaluronic acid results in appearance of dry and wrinkled skin.

Elastin is an insoluble elastic fibre present in extra cellular matrix and helps to maintain the elasticity and resilience of skin.[40] Elastin along with collagen maintain the mechanical strength of connective tissue. Elastase causes the degradation of elastin leading to the reduced elasticity of the skin, thereby resulting in sagging (figure 4).[41] Further the exposure to UV radiations or the release of cytokines results in the degradation of elastin fibres leading to wrinkles formation. [42]

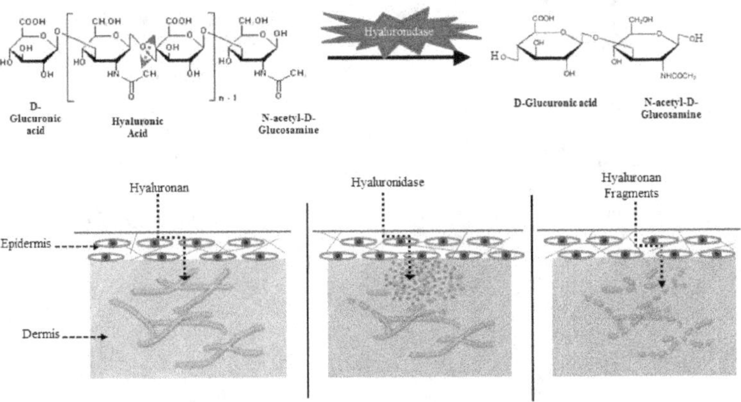

Figure 3: Schematic Pathway for the degradation of hyaluronic acid

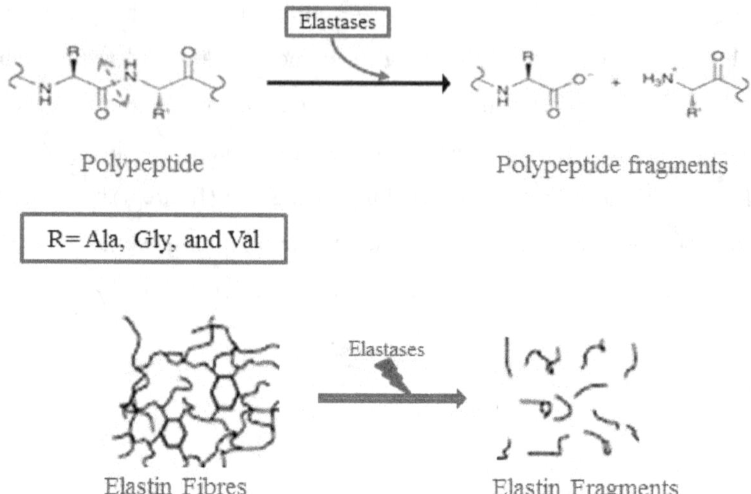

Figure 4: Schematic Pathway for the degradation of elastin fibers

Skin ageing

Skin ageing is a natural phenomenon and is characterized by the gradual loss of skin elasticity leading to sagging.[50]Coinciding slow wound healing with slow epidermal turnover rate and cell cycle lengthening, are the other most important characteristics of skin ageing.[51] Thus it is believed that the skin appearance improve with faster epidermal turnover rate which speed up the wound healing.[52] Further the dermal fibroblasts and epidermal keratinocytes of aged skin are characterized by the increased expression of senescence marker β-galactosidase, indicating more senescent cellsin aged skin.[59] Also, the microvasculature functioning reduces with ageing. This occurs due to endothelial dysfunction with impaired angiogenic capacity, abnormal expression of adhesion molecules, and reduced vasodilatory function.[67] Skin ageing is influenced by various endogenous or intrinsic and exogenous or extrinsic factors. The endogenous factors areintrinsic genetic or metabolic factors like cellular metabolism andhormone whileexogenous factors include exposure to light, pollution, ionizing radiation, chemicals and toxins.[43]

Intrinsic factors mainly cause intrinsic ageing such as the ageing of inner side of upper arm, whereas extrinsic factors, especially solar UV radiation, mainly cause ageing of the exposed skin areas.[56] Therefore the intrinsic ageing results in the development of the thin, dry skin, with fine wrinkles characterized by the gradual dermal atrophy, while the extrinsic ageing results in the development of the coarse wrinkles, loss of elasticity, laxity and rough-textured appearance.[54,55] The intrinsically aged skin is characterized by the significantchanges within the histology of basal cell layer such asthinning of the epidermis and shrinkages in the contact surface area between dermis and epidermis, therebythe exchangesurface for supplyingnutrition to the epidermis decreases and thus causes decrease basal cell proliferation.[57,58]

Extrinsic ageing mainly occurs due to the UV radiation exposure and accounts for about 80% of facial ageing.[60]Exposure to UV radiations particularly UV-B and UV-A has deleterious effects on the human skin which include sunburns, photoageing, immunosuppression, etc.[75-77] UV-A radiation is more harmful as they penetrate into deeper layers of the skin and provokes premature skin ageing. Thus, both UV-A and UV-B radiations are responsible for the various skin problems including photosensitivity, phototoxicity, photocarcinogenesis.[78-80]UV-irradiation also promotes elastolysis, resulting in the severe deposition of truncated elastic fibers [65,66] Particularly photo-ageing results in the formation of the thickened epidermis, mottled discoloration, deep wrinkles, laxity, dullness and roughness.[44-49, 61]This mostly affects the outmost layer of the epidermis called stratum corneum, which thickens due to failure in degradation of corneocyte desmosomes. This occurs due to the reduced expression of cell-surface protein β1-integrin(considered as one of the epidermal stem cell markers)which interacts with extracellular matrix proteins.[62,63] UV radiation exposure also causes the loss of fibrillin and collagen type VII resulting in theweakening of bond between dermis and epidermis resulting in wrinkles formation. [53,64]UV mediated generation of ROS increases the biosynthesis of melanin by inducing the proliferation of melanocytes responsible for colour changes in skin, ageing and wrinkling. [71-74] It is suggested that the UV radiations cause the production of reactive oxygen species (ROS) resulting in the inhibition of activity of receptor protein tyrosine phosphatases (RPTPs) by binding to cysteine in the catalytic sites of RPTPs, by elevating the level of phosphorylated RTKs and triggering downstream signaling pathways. It includes the activation of mitogen-activated protein kinase (MAPK) and subsequent nuclear factor-κB (NF-κB) and transcription factor activator protein-1 (AP-1). Activated NF-κB and AP-1 repress collagen production and increase MMP gene transcription, resulting in the decrease of collagen content in photoaged skin [68-70]. Besides this, AP-1 also inhibits TGF-β (transforming growth factor-β) signaling responsible for the decreased synthesis of procollagen type I and type III.[84,85] Further ROS also led to the activation of MAPKs, a family of proline-directed Ser/Thr kinases which comprises of ERKs (extracellular signal-regulated kinases which stimulates the expression of c-Fos), p38 and JNK (c-Jun NH 2-terminal kinase), both of which are important for the expression of c-Jun. Further, both c-Jun and c-Fos combine to form AP-1 (Activator Protein -1), which plays a key role in the up- regulation of MMP-1, MMP-3, and MMP-9 causing the degradation of collagen I and III (figure 5).[81-83, 86,87]

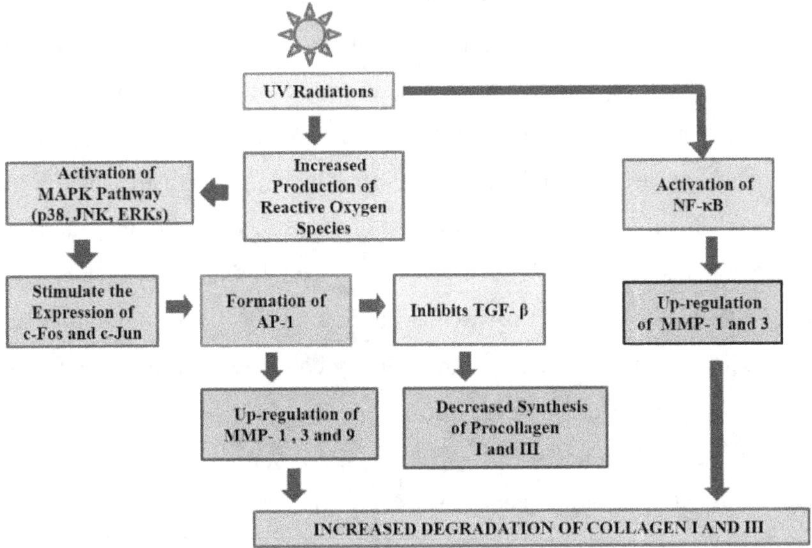

Figure 5: Damageing effects of UV radiations on skin

AGEs and their role in skin ageing

Glycation is a non- enzymatic reaction between proteins, lipids and nucleic acids with a reducing sugar such as glucose and fructose that generate advanced glycation end products (AGEs). AGEs are designed by Maillard reaction which involves the chemical reaction between the carbonyl group of reducing sugar (glucose) and a free amino group (mainly lysine and arginine) of proteins/ lipids/ nucleic acids non-enzymatically to form an unstable aldimine intermediate called Schiff base. This Schiff base then undergoes chemical rearrangement to form more stable Amadori product, known as early glycation products (hemoglobin A1c is the most well-known). This reaction is also reversible reaction. When Amadori product accumulates, they undergo irreversible chemical rearrangements like oxidation, dehydration, and polymerization and cross linking reactions to form very stable advanced glycation end products which are brownish and possess fluorescent properties.[91,92] In addition to, Maillard reaction, various other pathways are responsible for the formation of AGEs. These include autoxidation of glucose (Wolff Pathway), lipid peroxidation to form di-carbonyl α - oxaldehydes i.e. glyoxal, methylglyoxal and 3-deoxyglucosone which form AGEs on combining with monoacids, polyol pathway that involves the conversion of glucose into fructose via formation of sorbitol which is finally converted into di-carbonyl α-oxaldehydes leading to the formation of AGEs on interaction with monoacids (figure 9).[93-94] The most commonly analyzed AGEs employed as biomarkers for their *in- vivo* formation include pentosidine, pyrraline, carboxy methyl-lysine, and methylglyoxal.[95-97] AGEs form covalent cross-links with collagen leading to the degradation of collagen.[88,89] AGEs also damage elastin, and glycosaminoglycans which help to maintain the skin firmness, elasticity, and skin hydration responsible for the development of various deleterious effects such as uneven skin tone, brown patches, deep wrinkles, etc. Increased AGEs formation has been reported in diabetic patients susceptible to skin ageing. Therefore the inhibition of AGEs formation might prevent the characteristics of skin such as wrinkles.[90] The deleterious effects of AGEs on skin ageing are generally exerted by two different means: One is receptor independent which causes cross-linking of collagen and elastin and the other that receptor dependent (RAGE) (figure 8).[98] RAGE activates the action of the mitogen-activated protein kinases (MAPKs) which further activates transcription factor NF-κB (nuclear factor kappa B). NF-κB activation leads to an increase in the expression of RAGE, thus enhancing the formation of inflammation promoters. Besides age, RAGE is also responsible for the activation of NAD(P)H oxidase, which is responsible for production of superoxide. The up-regulation of this complex leads to increase in intracellular oxidative stress. An instant elevation in oxidative stress induced by NAD(P)H oxidase also activates NF-κB.[99-101]

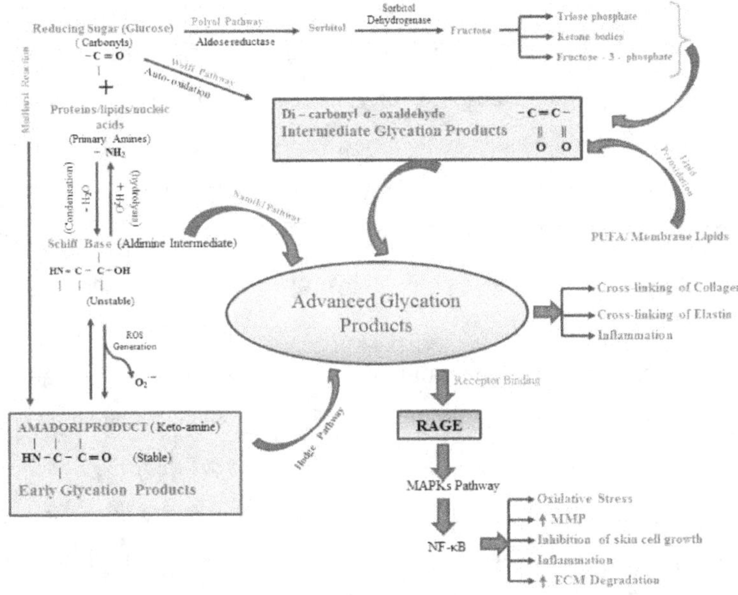

Figure 6: Role of AGEs in skin ageing

Role of reactive oxygen species in skin damage

Skin is most susceptible part of body which is prone to oxidative stress since it contains abundant proteins, lipids, carbohydrates and DNA which are highly affected by the oxidative processes and ROS generation.[102,03] ROS triggers peroxidation of lipids, causes mutations in DNA and disfigures the membrane proteins resulting in cutaneous ageing (figure 7).[104] Lipid peroxidation interferes with the liquidity of plasma membrane and the seepage of various molecules and thus hamper their key functions.[103,105]Excessive production of reactive oxygen species results in lipid peroxidation, which in turn increases the oxidative stress. The extent of lipid peroxidation is used as an index to measure the damage caused due to the production of reactive oxygen species.[110] The oxygen derived free radicals usually target two sites on phospholipid molecules, i.e. unsaturated carbon-carbon double bond (figure 8) and the ester linkage between glycerol and fatty acid. These peroxyl radicals are responsible for the peroxidation of polyunsaturated fatty acids (PUFA) present in phospholipid membranes. They start the chain reaction by abstracting a hydrogen atom from the side-chain methylene carbon of PUFA forming conjugated dienes, and hydroperoxides.[111] The lipid hydroperoxides are very unstable and easily decomposes to secondary products such as aldehydes like hexenals, malondialdehydes (MDA) and 4-hydroxynonenal.[112] Oxidative stress is also responsible for the transformation or loss of nitrogenous bases and rupture of DNA that may lead to serious effects.[105] Oxidative damage disrupts the fundamental structural configuration of skin resulting in the uneven, blotchy pigmentation, wrinkles and sagging.[106] Although, the skin itself has its own natural antioxidant defence mechanisms which act by scavenging the free radicals. Therefore, antioxidants play a vital role in protection and treatments of age-related diseases associated with the generation of free radicals.[107,108] Antioxidants donate an electron to free radicals and thereby reduces their reactivity (figure 9). There are various methods to evaluate an antioxidant potential of any given drug which can be referred separately from other reviews specifically on *in-vitro* techniques of the assay of antioxidants.[109] Here, in this review, only two *in-vitro* methods are discussed which are most commonly used.

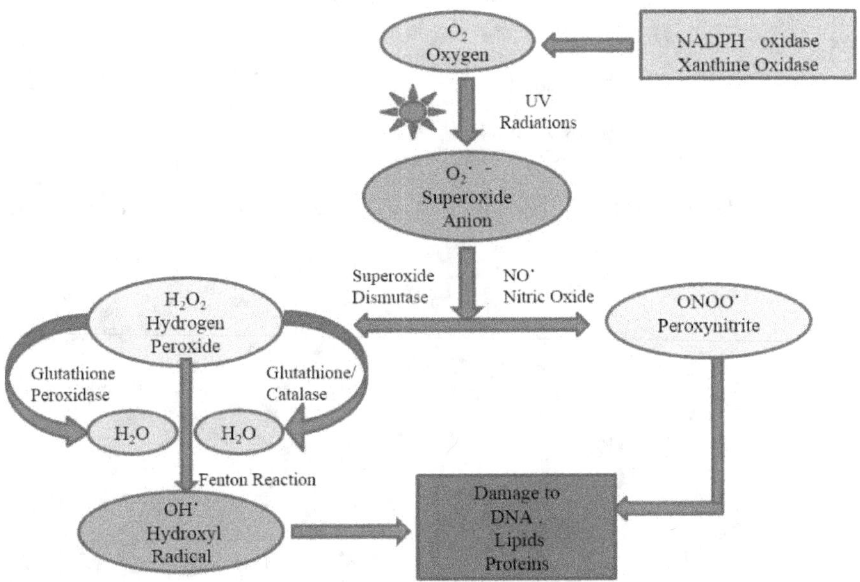

Figure 7: ROS mediated skin damage

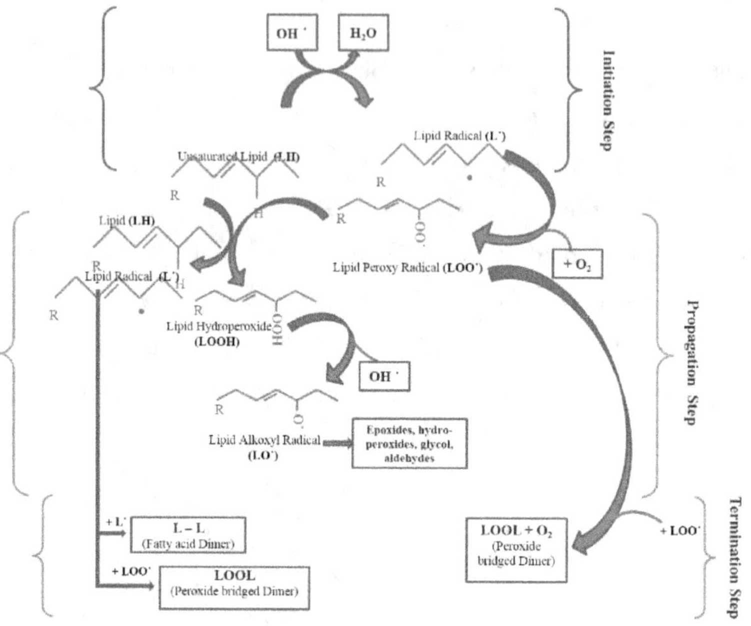

Figure 8: Lipid peroxidation and deleterious effect on cell membranes.

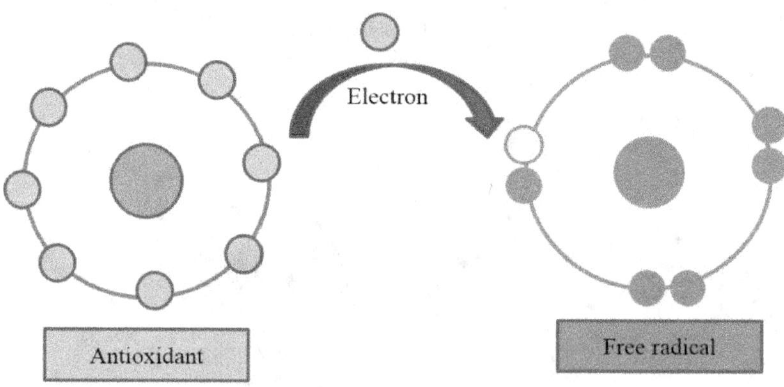

Figure 9: Antioxidant defense mechanism against skin ageing

In-vitro Assays

The skin ageing research and the evaluation of cosmetic products are specifically concerned for the use of animals for testing. Hence, in the interests of animal welfare, there is a need to reduce or avoid the animal experiments. Thus, the replacement of animal experiments with other alternative non- animal methods are gaining interests of the researchers as they have better perspectives in terms of time consumption, cost and improved experimental data quality. Moreover, the symptoms of skin ageing are very hard to notice on the animal skin.[113,114] Therefore, the present review mainly focuses on the *in-vitro* models of screening as they are more efficient with respect to time required to obtain the results, economical in expenditure and requires less human involvement as subjects for clinical trials. The proper and cautious selection of evaluating procedures and handling the experiments skilfully will provide the researchers with novel alternative methods for modern dermatology, cosmetic and skin ageing research.

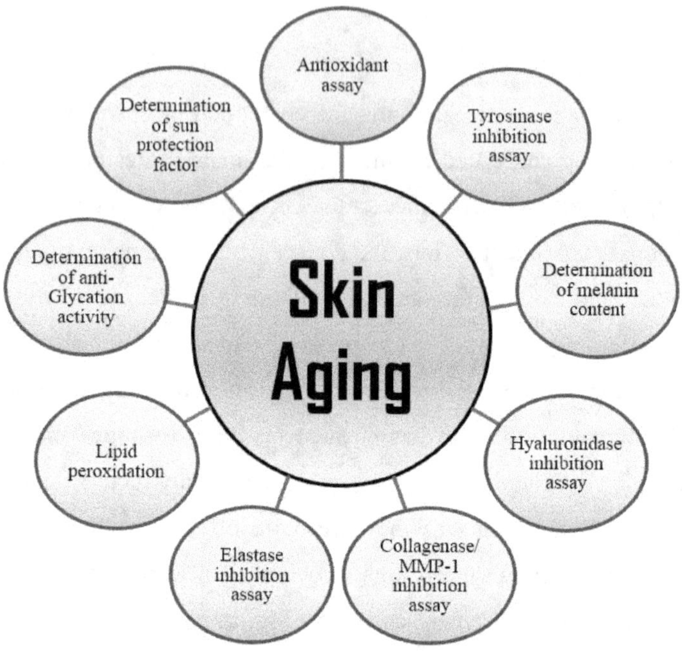

Figure 10: In-Vitro assays

1.   *1, 1 Diphenyl 2- picryl hydrazyl (DPPH) Assay*

DPPH is red in color in stable form and becomes yellow when it is scavenged by any antioxidant. The DPPH assay method utilizes this property to demonstrate the free radical scavenging activity. The scavenging potential of the antioxidant or extracts with regards to its hydrogen donating ability depends upon the intensity of discoloration. The change in optical density of DPPH is monitored to assess the antioxidant potential. [115-119] In this assay, the sample solutions of different concentrations are prepared followed by the addition of 1 ml of DPPH solution to them. The solution was then kept at room temperature for 30 min followed by the determination of absorbance at

517. Reference standard used in this experiment is ascorbic acid, and the analysis is carried out in triplicate. The following equation calculates the % DPPH scavenging effect or % inhibition:

$$DPPH + H- \longrightarrow (Yellow)$$

$$\text{Percentage inhibition} = A_0 - A_1 / A_0 \times 100.$$

Where A_0 is the control reaction absorbance, and A_1 is the test or standard sample absorbance.

2. *2, 2'-Azinobis-3-ethylbenzothiozoline-6-sulphonic acid (ABTS) Assay*

The test is based upon the principle that the ABTS radicals ($ABTS^{\cdot+}$) absorb the light of particular wavelength. The stable ABTS radicals are green in color and can be quantitatively estimated using spectrophotometric.[120,121] $ABTS^{\cdot+}$ reacts with ammonium persulphate to produce the blue, green colored $ABTS^{\cdot+}$ radicals which on reduction results in the absorbance loss. In this assay procedure, the solution containing $ABTS^{\cdot+}$ radicals is prepared by mixing 2.5 ml of 7 mM ABTS with 14.7 mM ammonium persulphate and kept in the dark for 16 hours at room temperature. In the next step, the sample solutions of different concentrations are prepared followed by the addition of 2 ml of $ABTS^{\cdot+}$ solution. The solution is kept undisturbed for about 30 min followed by the determination of absorbance at 734 nm.

Inhibition (%)   =   [(A Control – A Sample) /A Control] x 100

3.   *Tyrosinase inhibition assay*

The enzyme tyrosinase catalyses the transformation of L-tyrosine (monophenol) into 3, 4 – dihydroxyphenyl alanine or L-DOPA (o-diphenol) by hydroxylation which is further converted to o-dopaquinone (o-quinone) by oxidation. Then, through a series of enzymatic and non-enzymatic reactions o-dopaquinone is rapidly transformed into melanin.[122] In this assay procedure L-DOPA is used as the substrate.[123-126] Firstly, mix 0.8 ml of L-DOPA (2.5 mM) with 2.4 ml of 0.067 M phosphate buffer solution (PBS; pH 6.6) and incubate for 10 min at 37°C. In the next step, the sample solutions of different concentrations are prepared followed by the addition of 0.8 ml of tyrosinase solution to the mixture followed by the determination of the absorbance at 475 nm

$$\text{Inhibition (\%)} \quad \text{DPPH- H} + \text{A} \quad = \quad \frac{(C - D) - (A - D)}{C - D}$$

where A is absorbance measured with L-DOPA and sample, B is absorbance without L-DOPA but with sample, C is absorbance with substrate only deprived of sample, D is absorbance without samples and substrate.

4. *Melanin assay*

The test is based upon the fact that the UV radiation exposure increases the melanin content of the cells. To determine the effect of UV radiation exposure on the melanin content UV-A dose of 16 J/cm2 is used.[127] Firstly, the cells are solubilized in 1M NaOH and then about

200μl of each lysate are spectrophotometrically analyzed at 475 nm for the determination of the total melanin content. For obtaining melanin content per cell, a standard curve obtained using synthetic DOPA-melanin is employed. This assay accounts for the uptake of 14C-DOPA, an alternative method of evaluation of melanin synthesis.[128] The results obtained in each experiment are represented as a percentage of the melanin contents of untreated control cells because the basal melanin of melanocytes differs between melanocyte cultures.

5. *Lipid peroxidation assay*

Lipid peroxidation can be determined by measuring the amount of polyunsaturated fatty acids that breakdown to produce malondialdehyde (MDA). MDA recats with thiobarbituric acid (TBA) to gives pink color at 535 nm. In this assay procedure, 20 mg of egg phosphatidylcholine is dissolved in 2ml of chloroform and subjected to a rotary evaporator to get the dried, thin homogeneous film. Then, with the help of vortex mixer, it is dispersed in 5ml of normal saline. After that, the mixture is sonicated to get a uniform suspension of liposomes. Then, by adding ascorbic acid (0.05 mM) to the mixture containing 0.1 ml liposome, ferric chloride (0.2 mM), potassium chloride (150 mM) and sample solution of different concentration to produce a total volume of 0.4 ml. The reaction mixture so formed is incubated at 37°C for 40 min. The reaction was terminated by the addition of 1 ml of ice-cold 0.25M hydrochloric acid (containing trichloroacetic acid (20% w/v), butylated hydroxytoluene (0.05% w/v) and thiobarbituric acid (0.4% w/v). The samples are then heated at 80°C for 20 min and cooled. A constant volume of n-butanol is used to extract the pink colored chromogen, and the absorbance of the upper organic layer is estimated at 535 nm. [129]

6. Hyaluronidase inhibition assay

Hyaluronidase inhibition is estimated by measuring the amount of N-acetyl glucosamine splited from potassium hyaluronate. In this assay procedure, bovine hyaluronidase solution of concentration 1mg/ml is prepared by dissolving it in an acetate buffer (0.1M) of pH 3.5. Secondly, the sample solutions of different concentration are prepared. Add 50 µl of bovine hyaluronidase solution to 50 µl of sample solution, incubate at 37°C for 20 min followed by the addition of 50 µl of 12.5 mM calcium chloride and further incubation at 37°C for 20 min. The Ca^{2+} activated hyaluronidase obtained is then treated with 250 µl sodium hyaluronate (1.2mg/ml dissolved in 0.1 M acetate buffer, pH 3.5) and incubated at 37°C for 40 min. After 40 min, 100 µl of 0.2 M sodium borate and 50 µl of 0.4 M sodium hydroxide are added to the mixture and heat it on boiling water bath for 3 min followed by cooling to room temperature. Then 1.5 ml of p-dimethyl amino benzaldehyde solution (4gms PDMAB dissolved in 350 ml of glacial acetic acid) and 50 ml of 10 N HCl are added to the reaction mixture. Again, incubate the reaction mixture in a water bath at 37°C for 20 min followed by the determination of absorbance at 585nm [130]:

$$\text{Inhibition (\%)} = \left[\frac{\text{O.D of control - O.D of sample}}{\text{O.D of sample}} \right] \times 100$$

7. *Elastase Inhibition assay*

Elastase inhibition assay is performed according to the method described by Lee et al.[130] In elastase inhibition assay, "N-Succ-(Ala)$_3$-p-nitroanilide" is used as a substrate and elastase is assayed by determining the amount of p-nitroaniline so produced in the reaction.[131] The sample of the different concentrations are prepared followed by the addition of 1 ml of 0.2 M Tris-HCl buffer (pH 8.0), the volume is make upto 10 ml. 1 mg/ ml stock solution of pancreatic elastase is prepared by dissolving it in 0.2 M Tris-HCl buffer. The substrate N-Succinyl-Ala-Ala-Ala-p-nitroanilide (SANA) is also dissolved in buffer (0.8 mM). The final 250 µl reaction mixture consists of 160 µl buffer, 50 µl sample, 20 µl enzyme solution and 20 µl substrate. The solution is kept at room temperature for about 10 min followed by the determination of absorbance at 410 nm

$$\text{Inhibition (\%)} = [1 - (B / A)] \times 100$$

where, B is the Activity in presence of sample and A is the Enzyme activity without sample.

8. *Collagenase inhibition assay*

Collagenase inhibition assay is performed as per the method described by Kim et al.[89] Collagenase splits the X-Gly bond of collagen and synthetic peptides at sequence -Pro-X- Gly-Pro-, where X can be any amino acid, with blocked imino terminus. N-(3-[2-Furyl]acryloyl)-Leu-Gly-Pro-Ala (FALGPA) is used as a substrate and decrease in absorbance of the substrate after addition of enzyme.[132]0.8 units/ ml of Collagenase from *Clostridium histolyticum* and 2mM of FALGPA are used for carrying out the assay. Test solutions are prepared by using tricine buffer (50mM).[132,133] The final reaction mixture contains 25µl of 50 mM tricine buffer, 25µl of test extract and 25µl of *Clostridium histolyticum* collagenase enzyme, 50µl of 2mM FALGPA substrate. The reaction mixture was kept for 30 min followed by the determination of absorbance at 340 nm

$$\text{FALGPA} + \xrightarrow{\text{Collagenase}} \text{FAL} + \text{Gly - Pro - Ala}$$

$$\text{Percentage inhibition (\%)} = [1 - (B / A)] \times 100$$

where, A is the activity of enzyme and B is the activity in the presence of sample.

9. Antiglycation assay

For the detection and estimation of antiglycation activity, fluorescence spectroscopy is the best and most commonly used technique. The property of AGEs to exhibit a characteristic fluorescent spectrum at 440 nm subsequent to excitation at 370 nm is primary used to ascertain their agglomeration at tissue level.[134,135] Antiglycation activity is analyzed using the slight modification in bovine serum albumin assay.[136] In this assay procedure, 500µl of bovine serum albumin (1 mg/ml) is incubated with 400µl of glucose (500 mM) and 100µl of sample. The bovine serum albumin 500µl (1 mg/ml), 100µl saline phosphate buffer and 100µl sample, which serves a negative control, are also incubated under same conditions. The reaction is allowed to progress for 24 hours at 60 °C, and then 10µl of 100% (W/V) trichloroacetic acid (TCA) is added to stop the reaction. The above mixture with TCA, kept at 4 °C for 10 minutes, is centrifuged at 13000 rpm for 4 minutes. The precipitate obtained is then redissolved in phosphate buffer saline (pH 10), and Fluorescent Microplate Reader quantifies the relative amount of glycated bovine serum albumin. The excitation and emission wavelength used are at 370 nm and 440 nm respectively. Percentage inhibition is calculated using the following formula:

$$\text{Percentage inhibition} = \text{OD blank} - (\text{OD sample} - \text{OD sample negative}) / \text{OD blank} \times 100$$

10. Sun protection factor (SPF) determination

SPF indicates the protection against erythemally effective solar UV radiation, as the biological endpoint in SPF determination is the UV erythema.[137-141] SPF is the measure of UV energy essential for producing a MED (minimal erythema dose) on the protected skin to the UV energy required on unprotected skin. Minimal erythema dose (MED) is described as the dosage of UV light radiation or lowest time interval required to produce a minimum, perceptible erythema on unprotected skin.[142] Firstly, weigh 1.0g of sample and dilute it 100ml with ethanol, then ultrasonicate it for 5 min. After that filter it through cotton and reject the first 10ml. Take 5.0 ml of the above solution and dilute it to 50ml with ethanol. Then, again take 5.0 ml of this solution and make up the volume to 25ml with ethanol. Thereafter, determine the absorbance of each solution prepared at 5 nm interval from 290-320 nm, taking ethanol as a blank and multiply the absorbance values obtained with the respective EE (λ) values. Then, multiply their summation with the correction factor i.e. 10. Express the obtained data as mean $\pm$ S. The estimations are done in triplicate and the analysis is done at each point by applying Mansur equation. A very simple mathematical equation was developed by Mansur et al.[143] which substitutes the *in vitro* method given by Sayre et al.[144] utilizing UV Spectrophotometer.

Conclusion

Due to the increased demands of the methods which can be efficient, less tedious, more cost effective and involves less human participation, *in-vitro* models are considered as a rationale approach to carry out the evaluation. This review targets such evaluating parameters that may be helpful for the researchers to determine the major skin problems associated with the exposure to UV radiations. These may be either the sun burns or other photo damage which can be analyzed by estimating the antioxidant activity and the sun protection factor. The presence of hyper-pigmentation can be assessed by the carrying out the tyrosinase and melanin inhibitory assays. Skin elasticity, tensile strength and water holding capacity of the skin to keep it hydrated can be estimated by determining the elastase inhibition, anti-collagenase activity and hyaluronidase inhibition respectively. Furthermore, Anti-glycation activity can be used to determine the damage to collagen, elastin and glycosaminoglycans which help to maintain the skin firmness, elasticity and skin hydration. Thus, this article will help many researchers in developing new skin care formulations and products which will be safer and efficient.

References

1. Costin GE, Hearing VJ. Human skin pigmentation:melanocytes modulate skin color in response to stress. FASEB J Off Publ Fed Am Soc Exp Biol 2007;21:976-94.
2. Svobodova A, Walterova D, Vostalova J. Ultraviolet light induced alteration to the skin. Biomed Pap Med Fac Univ Palacky Olomouc Czechoslov 2006;150:25-38.

3. Rai R, Shanmuga SC, Srinivas C. Update on photoprotection. Indian J Dermatol 2012;57:335-42.

4. Hussein MR. Ultraviolet radiation and skin cancer : molecular mechanisms. J Cutan Pathol 2005;32:191-205.

5. Shehada A. A review on natural bioactive compounds as potential anti wrinkle agents. World J Pharm 2014;3:528-44.

6. Kuno N, Matsumoto M, inventors;Nisshin Oil Mills Ltd, assignee. Skin-beautifying agent, anti-ageing agent for the skin, whitening agent and external agent for the skin. United States patent US 6,682,763. 2004.

7. Afaq F, Mukhtar H. Effects of solar radiation on cutaneous detoxification pathways. J Photochem Photobiol B 2001;63:61-9.

8. Goihman-Yahr M. Skin ageing and photoageing:an outlook. Clin Dermatol 1996;14:153-60.

9. Lucas RM, McMichael AJ, Armstrong BK, SmithWT. Estimating the global disease burden due to ultraviolet radiation exposure. Int J Epidemiol 2008;37:654-67.

10. Fisher GJ, Kang S, Varani J, Bata-Csorgo Z, Wan Y, Datta S, et al. Mechanisms of photoageing and chronological skin ageing. Arch Dermatol 2002;138:1462-70.

11. Bosch R, Philips N, Jorge A, Suárez-Pérez, Juarranz A, Devmurari A, Chalensouk-Khaosaat J, et al. Mechanisms of Photoageing and Cutaneous Photocarcinogenesis, and Photoprotective Strategies with Phytochemicals. Antioxidants 2015;4:248-68.

12. Elmets CA, Anderson CY. Sunscreens and photocarcinogenesis:an objective assessment. Photochem Photobiol 1996;63:435-40.

13. Thring TSA, Hili P, Naughton DP. Anti-collagenase, anti-elastase and anti-oxidant activities of extracts from 21 plants. BMC Complement Altern Med 2009;9:27.

14. Wen KC, Fan PC, Tsai SY, Shih IC, Chiang HM. Ixora parviflora Protects against UVB-Induced Photoageing by Inhibiting the Expression of MMPs, MAP Kinases, and COX-2 and by Promoting Type I Procollagen Synthesis. Evid-Based Complement Altern Med ECAM 2012;2012:417346.

15. Chiang HM, Chen HC, Lin TJ, Shih IC, Wen KC. Michelia alba extract attenuates UVB-induced expression of matrix metalloproteinases via MAP kinase pathway in human dermal fibroblasts. Food Chem Toxicol Int J Publ Br Ind Biol Res Assoc 2012;50:4260- 9.

16. Chiang HM, Chen HC, Chiu HH, Chen CW, Wang SM, Wen KC. Neonauclea reticulata (Havil.) Merr Stimulates Skin Regeneration after UVB Exposure via ROS Scavenging and Modulation of the MAPK/MMPs/Collagen Pathway. Evid Based Complement Alternat Med 2013;2013:1-9.

17. Ham SA, Kang ES, Lee H, Hwang JS, Yoo T, Paek KS, et al. PPARδ inhibits UVB-induced secretion of MMP-1 through MKP-7-mediated suppression of JNK signaling. J Invest Dermatol 2013;133:2593 - 600.

18. Steinbrenner H, Ramos MC, Stuhlmann D, Sies H, Brenneisen P. UVA-mediated downregulation of MMP-2 and MMP-9 in human epidermal keratinocytes. Biochem Biophys Res Commun 2003;308:486-91.

19. Kim J, Lee CW, Kim EK, Lee SJ, Park NH, Kim HS, Kim HK, Char K, Jang YP, Kim JW. Inhibition effect of Gynura

procumbens extract on UV-B-induced matrix-metalloproteinase expression in human dermal fibroblasts. Journal of ethnopharmacology. 2011;137:427-33.

20. Jung SK, Lee KW, Kim HY, Oh MH, Byun S, Lim SH, et al. Myricetin suppresses UVB-induced wrinkle formation and MMP-9 expression by inhibiting Raf. Biochem Pharmacol 2010;79:1455 - 61.

21. Wang Y, Chen H, Wang W, Wang R, Liu Z-L, Zhu W, et al. N-terminal 5-mer peptide analog P165 of amyloid precursor protein inhibits UVA-induced MMP-1 expression by suppressing the MAPK pathway in human dermal fibroblasts. Eur J Pharmacol 2014;734:1- 8.

22. Seo SY, Sharma VK, Sharma N. Mushroom Tyrosinase:Recent Prospects. J Agric Food Chem 2003;51:2837-53.

23. Perluigi M, De Marco F, Foppoli C, Coccia R, Blarzino C, Marcante ML, et al. Tyrosinase protects human melanocytes from ROS-generating compounds. Biochem Biophys Res Commun 2003;305:250-6.

24. Lin JY, Fisher DE. Melanocyte biology and skin pigmentation. Nature 2007;445:843-50.

25. Hanamura T, Uchida E, Aoki H. Skin-lightening effect of a polyphenol extract from Acerola (Malpighia emarginata DC.) fruit on UV-induced pigmentation. Biosci Biotechnol Biochem 2008;72:3211-8.

26. Wang K-H, Lin R-D, Hsu F-L, Huang Y-H, Chang H-C, Huang C-Y, et al. Cosmetic applications of selected traditional Chinese herbal medicines. J Ethnopharmacol 2006;106:353-9.

27. Pilawa B, Buszman E, Latocha M, Wilczok T. Free Radicals in DOPA-melanin-chloroquine Complexes. Pol J Med Phys Eng 2006;10.

28. del Marmol V, Beermann F. Tyrosinase and related proteins in mammalian pigmentation. FEBS Lett 1996;381:165-8.

29. Langfelder K, Streibel M, Jahn B, Haase G, Brakhage AA. Biosynthesis of fungal melanins and their importance for human pathogenic fungi. Fungal Genet Biol 2003;38:143-58.

30. Baumann L. Skin ageing and its treatment. J Pathol 2007;211:241-51.

31. Toole BP. Hyaluronan:from extracellular glue to pericellular cue. Nat Rev Cancer 2004;4:528-39.

32. Papakonstantinou E, Karakiulakis G, Roth M, Block LH. Platelet-derived growth factor stimulates the secretion of hyaluronic acid by proliferating human vascular smooth muscle cells. Proc Natl Acad Sci U S A 1995;92:9881-5.

33. Papakonstantinou E, Roth M, Tamm M, Eickelberg O, Perruchoud AP, Karakiulakis G. Hypoxia differentially enhances the effects of transforming growth factor-beta isoforms on the synthesis and secretion of glycosaminoglycans by human lung fibroblasts. J Pharmacol Exp Ther 2002;301:830-7.

34. Papakonstantinou E, Kouri FM, Karakiulakis G, Klagas I, Eickelberg O. Increased hyaluronic acid content in idiopathic pulmonary arterial hypertension. Eur Respir J 2008;32:1504-12.

35. Klagas I, Goulet S, Karakiulakis G, Zhong J, Baraket M, Black JL, et al. Decreased hyaluronan in airway smooth muscle cells from patients with asthma and COPD. Eur Respir J 2009;34:616 -28.

36. Lee JY, Spicer AP. Hyaluronan:a multifunctional, megaDalton, stealth molecule. Curr Opin Cell Biol 2000;12:581-6.

37. Juhlin L. Hyaluronan in skin. J Intern Med 1997;242:61- 6.

38. Laurent TC, Fraser JR. Hyaluronan. FASEB J Off Publ Fed Am Soc Exp Biol 1992;6:2397- 404.

39. Tammi R, Ripellino JA, Margolis RU, Tammi M. Localization of epidermal hyaluronic acid using the hyaluronate binding region of cartilage proteoglycan as a specific probe. J Invest Dermatol 1988;90:412 - 4.

40. Oikarinen A. Connective tissue and ageing. Int J Cosmet Sci 2004;26:107- 107.

41. Antonicelli F, Bellon G, Debelle L, Hornebeck W. Elastin-elastases and inflamm-ageing. Curr Top Dev Biol 2007;79:99-155.

42. Nishimori Y, Kenjoh Y, Matsumoto K, Kawai M. UV-B induced ultrastructural changes of collagen bundles in hairless mouse skin. J Dermatol Sci 1997;15:125.

43. Cevenini E, Invidia L, Lescai F, Salvioli S, Tieri P, Castellani G, et al. Human models of ageing and longevity. Expert Opin Biol Ther. 2008;8:1393–405.

44. Kligman LH. Photoageing. Manifestations, prevention, and treatment. Clin Geriatr Med. 1989;5:235–51.

45. El-Domyati M, Attia S, Saleh F, Brown D, Birk DE, Gasparro F, et al. Intrinsic ageing vs. photoageing: a comparative histopathological, immunohistochemical, and ultrastructural study of skin. Exp Dermatol. 2002;11:398–405.

46. Moragas A, Castells C, Sans M. Mathematical morphologic analysis of ageing-related epidermal changes. Anal Quant CytolHistol. 1993;15:75–82.

47. Lock-Andersen J, Therkildsen P, de Fine Olivarius F, Gniadecka M, Dahlstrøm K, Poulsen T, et al. Epidermal thickness, skin pigmentation and constitutive photosensitivity. PhotodermatolPhotoimmunolPhotomed. 1997;13:153–8.

48. Makrantonaki E, Zouboulis CC. William J. Cunliffe Scientific Awards. Characteristics and pathomechanisms of endogenously aged skin. Dermatology. 2007;214:352–60. doi:10.1159/000100890.

49. Makrantonaki E, Zouboulis CC. Molecular mechanisms of skin ageing: state of the art. Ann N Y Acad Sci. 2007;1119:40–50.

50. Escoffier C, de Rigal J, Rochefort A, Vasselet R, Lévêque JL, Agache PG. Age-related mechanical properties of human skin: an in vivo study. J Invest Dermatol. 1989;93:353–7.

51. Yaar M, Gilchrest BA. Ageing of skin. In Fitzpatrick's Dermatology in General Medicine Vol 2, 5th edn. McGraw-Hill:New York, 1999; 1697–1706.

52. Baumann L. Skin ageing and its treatment. J Pathol. 2007;211:241–51.

53. Watson RE, Craven NM, Kang S, Jones CJ, Kielty CM, Griffiths CE. A short-term screening protocol, using fibrillin-1 as a reporter molecule, for photoageing repair agents. J Invest Dermatol. 2001;116:672–8.

54. Krutmann J, Bouloc A, Sore G, Bernard BA, Passeron T. The skin ageing exposome. J Dermatol Sci. 2017;85(3):152–161.

55. Mora Huertas AC, Schmelzer CE, Hoehenwarter W, Heyroth F, Heinz A. Molecular-level insights into ageing processes of skin elastin. Biochimie 2016;128–129:163–173.

56. Mancini M, Lena AM, Saintigny G, Mahe C, Di Daniele N, Melino G, Candi E. MicroRNAs in human skin ageing. Ageing Res Rev. 2014;17:9–15.

57. Makrantonaki E, Zouboulis CC, William J. Cunliffe Scientific Awards. Characteristics and pathomechanisms of endogenously aged skin. Dermatology. 2007;214(4):352–360.

58. Moragas A, Castells C, Sans M. Mathematical morphologic analysis of ageing-related epidermal changes. Anal Quant CytolHistol. 1993;15(2):75–82.

59. Dimri GP, Lee X, Basile G, Acosta M, Scott G, Roskelley C, Medrano EE, Linskens M, Rubelj I, Pereira-Smith O, et al. A biomarker that identifies senescent human cells in culture and in ageing skin in vivo. Proc Natl Acad Sci U S A. 1995;92(20):9363–9367.

60. Friedman O. Changes associated with the ageing face. Facial PlastSurg Clin North Am. 2005;13(3):371–380.

61. Kligman LH. Photoageing. Manifestations, prevention, and treatment. Clin Geriatr Med. 1989;5(1):235–251.

62. Bosset S, Bonnet-Duquennoy M, Barre P, Chalon A, Lazou K, Kurfurst R, Bonte F, Schnebert S, Disant F, Le Varlet B, et al. Decreased expression of keratinocyte beta1 integrins in chronically sun-exposed skin in vivo. Br J Dermatol. 2003;148(4):770–778.

63. Makrantonaki E, Zouboulis CC. Molecular mechanisms of skin ageing: state of the art. Ann N Y Acad Sci. 2007;1119:40–50.

64. Contet-Audonneau JL, Jeanmaire C, Pauly G. A histological study of human wrinkle structures: comparison between sun-exposed

areas of the face, with or without wrinkles, and sun-protected areas. Br J Dermatol. 1999;140(6):1038–1047.

65. Bonta M, Daina L, Mutiu G. The process of ageing reflected by histological changes in the skin. Rom J MorpholEmbryol. 2013;54(Suppl 3):797–804.

66. Bernstein EF, Chen YQ, Kopp JB, Fisher L, Brown DB, Hahn PJ, Robey FA, Lakkakorpi J, Uitto J. Long-term sun exposure alters the collagen of the papillary dermis. Comparison of sun-protected and photoaged skin by northern analysis, immunohistochemical staining, and confocal laser scanning microscopy. J Am Acad Dermatol. 1996;34(2 Pt 1):209–218.

67. Scioli MG, Bielli A, Arcuri G, Ferlosio A, Orlandi A. Ageing and microvasculature. Vasc Cell. 2014;6:19.

68. Rittie L, Fisher GJ. Natural and sun-induced ageing of human skin. Cold Spring HarbPerspect Med. 2015;5(1):a015370.

69. Kammeyer A, Luiten RM. Oxidation events and skin ageing. Ageing Res Rev. 2015;21:16–29.

70. Choi YJ, Moon KM, Chung KW, Jeong JW, Park D, Kim DH, Yu BP, Chung HY. The underlying mechanism of proinflammatory NF-κB activation by the mTORC2/Akt/IKKalpha pathway during skin ageing. Oncotarget. 2016;7(33):52685–52694.

71. Herrling T, Jung K, Fuchs J. The role of melanin as protector against free radicals in skin and its role as free radical indicator in hair. Spectrochim Acta A Mol Biomol Spectrosc 2008;69:1429-35.

72. Iida K, Hase K, Shimomura K, Sudo S, Kadota S, Namba T. Potent inhibitors of tyrosinase activity and melanin biosynthesis from Rheum officinale. Planta Med 1995;61:425-8.

73. Pawelek JM, Körner AM. The biosynthesis of mammalian melanin. Am Sci 1982;70:136-45.

74. Yamakoshi J, Otsuka F, Sano A, Tokutake S, Saito M, Kikuchi M, et al. Lightening effect on ultraviolet-induced pigmentation of guinea pig skin by oral administration of a proanthocyanidin-rich extract from grape seeds. Pigment Cell Res 2003;16:629-38.

75. Afaq F, Katiyar SK. Polyphenols:skin photoprotection and inhibition of photocarcinogenesis. Mini Rev Med Chem 2011;11:1200-15.

76. Katiyar SK. UV-induced immune suppression and photocarcinogenesis:Chemoprevention by dietary botanical agents. Cancer Lett 2007;255:1-11.

77. Pissavini M, Alard V, Heinrich U, Jenni K, Perier V, Tournier V, et al. In vitro assessment of water resistance of sun care products:a reproducible and optimized in vitro test method. Int J Cosmet Sci 2007;29:451-60.

78. Ferrero L, Pissavini M, Marguerie S, Zastrow L. Sunscreen in vitro spectroscopy:application to UVA protection assessment and correlation with in vivo persistent pigment darkening. Int J Cosmet Sci 2002;24:63-70.

79. Bendová H, Akrman J, Krejčí A, Kubáč L, Jírová D, Kejlová K, et al. In vitro approaches to evaluation of Sun Protection Factor. Toxicol In Vitro 2007;21:1268-75.

80. Wood C, Murphy E. Sunscreen Efficacy. Glob Cosmet Ind 2000;167:38-43.

81. Kim J, Lee CW, Kim EK, Lee SJ, Park NH, Kim HS, Kim HK, Char K, Jang YP, Kim JW. Inhibition effect of Gynura procumbens extract on UVB-induced matrix-metalloproteinase

expression in human dermal fibroblasts. J. Ethnopharmacol. 2011, 137, 427-433.

82. Chiang HM, Chen HC, Chiu HH, Chen CW, Wang SM, Wen KC. Neonauclea reticulata (Havil.) merr stimulates skin regeneration after UVB exposure via ROS scavenging and modulation of the MAPK/MMPs/collagen pathway. Evid. Based Complement. Altern. Med. 2013;2013:1-9.

83. Park JE, Pyun HB, Woo SW, Jeong JH, Hwang JK. The protective effect of Kaempferia parviflora extract on UVB-induced skin photoageing in hairless mice. Photodermatol Photoimmunol Photomed 2014;30:237-45.

84. Sun ZW, Hwang E, Lee HJ, Lee TY, Song HG, Park SY, Shin HS, Lee DG, Yi TH. Effects of Galla chinensis extracts on UVB-irradiated MMP-1 production in hairless mice. J Nat Med 2015;69:22-34.

85. Chen B, Li R, Yan N, Chen G, Qian W, Jiang HL, Ji C, Bi ZG. Astragaloside IV controls collagen reduction in photoageing skin by improving transforming growth factor-β/Smad signaling suppression and inhibiting matrix metalloproteinase-1. Mol Med Rep 2015;11:3344-8.

86. Lee YR, Noh EM, Han JH, Kim JM, Hwang JK, Hwang BM, Chung EY, Kim BS, Lee SH, Lee SJ, et al. Brazil in inhibits UVB-induced MMP-1/3 expressions and secretions by suppressing the NF-κB pathway in human dermal fibroblasts. Eur J Pharmacol 2012:674:80-6.

87. Vicentini FTMC, He T, Shao Y, Fonseca MJV, Verri WA Jr, Fisher GJ, Xu Y. Quercetin inhibits UV irradiation-induced

inflammatory cytokine production in primary human keratinocytes by suppressing NF-κB pathway. J Dermatol Sci 2011;61:162-8.

88. Lee Y, Hong CO, Nam MH, Kim JH, Ma Y, Kim YB, et al. Antioxidant and glycation inhibitory activities of gold kiwifruit, Actinidia chinensis. J Korean Soc Appl Biol Chem 2011;54:460-7.

89. Pageon H. Reaction of glycation and human skin:the effects on the skin and its components, reconstructed skin as a model. Pathol Biol (Paris) 2010;58:226-31.

90. Jedsadayanmata A. In vitro antiglycation activity of arbutin. Naresuan Univ J 2005;13:35-41.

91. Brownlee M, Vlassara H, Cerami A. Nonenzimatic glycosilation and the pathogenesis of diabetes complications. Ann Intern Med 1984;101:527-37.

92. Ahmed, N. Advanced glycation end products - role in pathology of diabetic complications. Diabetes Res Clin Pract 2005;67:3-21.

93. Uribarri J, Tuttle KR. Advanced glycation end products and nephrotoxicity of high-protein diets. Clin J Am Soc Nephrol 2006;1:1293-9.

94. Lorenzi, M. The polyol pathway as a mechanism for diabetic retinopathy:Attractive, elusive, and resilient. Exp Diabetes Res 2007;2007:61038.

95. Ahmed N, Thornalley PJ. Quantitative screening of protein biomarkers of early glycation, advanced glycation, oxidation and nitrosation in cellular and extracellular proteins by tandem mass spectrometry multiple reaction monitoring. Biochem Soc Trans 2003;31:1417-22.

96. Oya T, Hattori N, Mizuno Y, Miyata S, Maeda S, Osawa T, Uchida K. Methyl glyoxal modification of protein. Chemical and

immunochemical characterization of methyl glyoxal-arginine adducts. J Biol Chem 1999;274:18492-502.

97. Cho SJ, Roman G, Yeboah F, Konishi Y. The road to advanced glycation end products:A mechanistic perspective. Curr Med Chem 2007;14:1653-71.

98. Sheetz MJ, King GL. Molecular understanding of hyperglycemia's adverse effects for diabetic complications. JAMA 2002;288:2579-88.

99. Basta G, Lazzerini G, Del TS, Ratto GM, Schmidt AM, De CR. At least 2 distinct pathways generating reactive oxygen species mediate vascular cell adhesion molecule-1 induction by advanced glycation end products. Arterioscler Thromb Vasc Biol 2005;25:1401-7.

100. Wautier MP, Chappey O, Corda S, Stern DM, Schmidt AM, Wautier JL. Activation of NADPH oxidase by AGE links oxidant stress to altered gene expression via RAGE. Am J Physiol Endocrinol Metab 2001;280:E685-94.

101. Lin L, Park S, Lakatta EG. RAGE signaling in inflammation and arterial ageing. Front Biosci 2009;14,1403-13

102. Silva AR, Menezes PFC, Martinello T, Novakovich GFL, Praes CEO, Feferman IHS. Antioxidant kinetics of plant-derived substances and extracts. Int J Cosmet Sci 2010;32:73-80.

103. Stadtman ER. Protein oxidation and ageing. Free Radic Res 2006;40(12):1250-8.

104. Chidambaram U, Pachamuthu V, Natarajan S, Elango B, Suriyanarayanan, Ramkumar KM. In vitro evaluation of free radical scavenging activity of Codariocalyx motorius root extract. Asian Pac J Trop Med 2013;6:188-94.

105. Kohen R. Skin antioxidants:their role in ageing and in oxidative stress--new approaches for their evaluation. Biomed Pharmacother Biomedecine Pharmacother 1999;53:181-92.

106. Fisher GJ, Quan T, Purohit T, Shao Y, Cho MK, He T, et al. Collagen fragmentation promotes oxidative stress and elevates matrix metalloproteinase-1 in fibroblasts in aged human skin. Am J Pathol 2009;174:101-14.

107. Gasca CA, Cabezas FA, Torras L, Bastida J, Codina C. Chemical composition and antioxidant activity of the ethanol extract and purified fractions of cadillo (Pavonia sepioides). Free Radic Antioxid 2013;3:55-61.

108. Kohen R, Gati I. Skin low molecular weight antioxidants and their role in ageing and in oxidative stress. Toxicology 2000;148:149-57.

109. Joseph NM, Monika S, Shashi A, Mahor A, Shruti R. *In-vitro* and *in-vivo* models for antioxidant activity evaluation:a review. International journal of pharmaceutical sciences and research 2010;1:1-11.

110. Sharma P, Jha AB, Dubey RS, Pessarakli M. Reactive Oxygen Species, Oxidative Damage, and Antioxidative Defense Mechanism in Plants under Stressful Conditions. J Bot 2012;2012:1-26.

111. Smirnoff N. Antioxidant Systems and Plant Response to the Environment. In:Environment and Plant Metabolism:Flexibility and Acclimation. Oxford:BIOS Scientific Publishers, 1995:217-43.

112. Davies KJ. Oxidative stress, antioxidant defenses, and damage removal, repair, and replacement systems. IUBMB Life 2000;50:279-89.

113. Tannenbaum J, Bennett BT. Russell and Burch's 3Rs Then and Now:The Need for Clarity in Definition and Purpose. Journal o9f American Association for Laboratory Animal Science 2015;54:120-32.

114. Bracken MB. Why animal studies are often poor predictors of human reactions to exposure. Journal of royal society of medicine 2009;102, 120-122.

115. Alam MN, Bristi NJ, Rafiquzzaman M. Review on in vivo and in vitro methods evaluation of antioxidant activity. Saudi Pharm J SPJ Off Publ Saudi Pharm Soc 2013;21:143-52.

116. M Ahmed, Saeed F, Mansoor M, Noor J. Evaluation of Insecticidal and Antioxidant activity of selected Medicinal plants. J Pharmacog Phytochem 2013;2:153-8.

117. Patel R, Patel N. *In vitro* antioxidant activity of coumarin compounds by DPPH, superoxide and nitric oxide free radical scavenging methods. J adv Pharm Edu Res 2011;1:52-68.

118. Koleva II, van Beek TA, Linssen JPH, de Groot A, Evstatieva LN. Screening of plant extracts for antioxidant activity:a comparative study on three testing methods. Phytochem Anal PCA 2002;13:8-17.

119. Achola KJ, Munenge RW. Bronchodilating and Uterine Activities of Ageratum conyzoides Extract. Pharm Biol 1998;36:93-6.

120. Jain PK, Agrawal RK. Antioxidant and Free Radical Scavenging Properties of Developed Mono- and Polyherbal Formulations. Asian J Exp Sci 2008;22:213-20.

121. Re R, Pellegrini N, Proteggente A, Pannala A, Yang M, Rice-Evans C. Antioxidant activity applying an improved ABTS radical cation decolorization assay. Free Radic Biol Med 1999;26:1231-7.

122. Prota G. Melanins and melanogenesis. San Diego:Academic Press;1992.

123. Jiménez M, Chazarra S, Escribano J, Cabanes J, García-Carmona F. Competitive inhibition of mushroom tyrosinase by 4-substituted benzaldehydes. J Agric Food Chem 2001;49:4060-3.

124. Hsu C, Chang C, Lu H, Chung Y. Inhibitory effects of the water extracts of Lavendula sp. on mushroom tyrosinase activity. Food Chem 2007;105:1099-105.

125. Wang B-S, Chang L-W, Wu H-C, Huang S-L, Chu H-L, Huang M-H. Antioxidant and antityrosinase activity of aqueous extracts of green asparagus. Food Chem 2011;127:141-6.

126. Kubo I, Kinst-Hori I. Tyrosinase inhibitory activity of the olive oil flavor compounds. J Agric Food Chem 1999;47:4574-8.

127. Carsberg CJ, Warenius HM, Friedmann PS. Ultraviolet radiation-induced melanogenesis in human melanocytes. Effects of modulating protein kinase C. J Cell Sci 1994;107:2591-7.

128. Friedmann PS, Gilchrest BA. Ultraviolet radiation directly induces pigment production by cultured human melanocytes. J Cell Physiol 1987;133:88-94.

129.Mantena SK, Jagadish null, Badduri SR, Siripurapu KB, Unnikrishnan MK. In vitro evaluation of antioxidant properties of Cocos nucifera Linn. water. Nahr 2003;47:126-31.

130.Lee KK, Kim JH, Cho JJ, Choi JD. Inhibitory Effects of 150 Plant Extracts on Elastase Activity, and Their Anti-inflammatory Effects. Int J Cosmet Sci 1999;21:71- 82.

131.Lee KK, Choi JD. The effects of areca catechu L extract on anti-ageing. Int J Cosmet Sci 1999;21:285 - 95.

132.Van Wart HE, Steinbrink DR. A continuous spectrophotometric assay for Clostridium histolyticum collagenase. Anal Biochem 1981;113:356-65.

133.Kim YJ, Uyama H, Kobayashi S. Inhibition effects of (+)-catechin-aldehyde polycondensates on proteinases causing proteolytic degradation of extracellular matrix. Biochem Biophys Res Commun 2004;320:256-61.

134.Akhter F, Salman Khan M, Shahab U, Moinuddin null, Ahmad S. Bio-physical characterization of ribose induced glycation:a mechanistic study on DNA perturbations. Int J Biol Macromol 2013;58:206-10.

135.Uribarri J, Peppa M, Cai W, Goldberg T, Lu M, Baliga S, et al. Dietary glycotoxins correlate with circulating advanced glycation end product levels in renal failure patients. Am J Kidney Dis Off J Natl Kidney Found 2003;42(3):532- 8.

136.Matsuura N, Aradate T, Sasaki C, Kojima H, Ohara M, Hasegawa J, et al. Screening System for the Maillard Reaction Inhibitor from Natural Product Extracts. J Health Sci - J Health Sci 2002;48:520- 6.

137. Ullrich SE. Mechanisms underlying UV-induced immune suppression. Mutat Res 2005;571:185-205.

138. Boniol M, Autier P, Doré J-F. Photoprotection. Lancet Lond Eng 2007;370:1481- 2.

139. Hojerová J, Medovcíková A, Mikula M. Photoprotective efficacy and photostability of fifteen sunscreen products having the same label SPF subjected to natural sunlight. Int J Pharm 2011;408:27-38.

140. Stanfield J, Osterwalder U, Herzog B. In vitro measurements of sunscreen protection. Photochem Photobiol Sci Off J Eur Photochem Assoc Eur Soc Photobiol 2010;9:489-94.

141. Kaur DCD, Saraf PS. Photochemoprotective Activity Of Alcoholic Extract Of Camellia sinensis. Int J Pharmacol 2011;7:400-4.

142. Wolf R, Wolf D, Morganti P, Ruocco V. Sunscreens. Clin Dermatol 2001;19:452-9.

143. Mansur J, Breder M, Mansur M, Azulay R. Determination of sun protection factor by spectrophotometry. Bras Dermatol 1986;61:121-4.

144. Sayre RM, Agin PP, LeVee GJ, Marlowe E. Comparison of in vivo and in vitro testing of sunscreens formulas. Photochem Photobiol 1979;29:559-66. 145.

Evaluation of anti-ageing and anti-wrinkle potential of *Oscimum tenuiflorum* L. through various enzymatic assays

Chanchal Garg, Amit Kumar, Sukender Kumar, Munish Garg

Abstract

Objective: To screen *Ocimum tenuiflorum*leaves extract for anti-ageing and antiwrinkle potential by *in-vitro* estimation of inhibition of enzymes that play an important role in maintaining the flexibility, elasticity, and strength of the skin, thus preventing or controlling skin ageing.

Materials and Methods: Dried leaves of *Ocimum tenuiflorum* were heated with water and fractionated with ethyl acetate and n-butanol. The obtained extracts were evaluatedfor their antioxidant potential through DPPH radical scavenging assay taking ascorbic acid as positive control and *in-vitro* enzyme inhibitory activities were evaluated especially in regards to hyaluronidase inhibition, matrix metalloproteinase-1 / collagenase inhibition, elastase inhibition, and tyrosinase inhibition assay. All the evaluations were performed in triplicates by spectrophotometric methods (using ELISA reader).

Statistical analysis: Linear regression was used to analyze the results which were expressed as the half-maximal inhibitory concentration (IC_{50}) of various drug extracts.

Results: It was observed that ethyl acetate extract of *Ocimum tenuiflorum*leaves showed a maximum DPPH radical scavenging activity (IC$_{50}$: 52.7µg/ml). The n- butanol fraction of *Ocimum tenuiflorum*leaves exhibited maximum matrix-metalloproteinase-1 / collagenase inhibitory activity and hyaluronidase inhibitory activity (IC$_{50}$: 42.16µg/ml and 58.57µg/ml respectively). Whereas, the aqueous extract of *Ocimum tenuiflorum*leaves showed the maximum tyrosinase as well as elastase inhibitory activity (IC$_{50}$: 28.38µg/ml and 25.74µg/ml respectively).

Conclusion: The antioxidant and enzyme inhibition activity of *Ocimum tenuiflorum*extracts have demonstrated significant anti-ageing and antiwrinkle properties that may prove it, a potential agent for various skincare products in the cosmetic industry.

Keywords: Anti-ageing, Antiwrinkle, *Ocimum tenuiflorum*, Hyaluronidase, Elastase, MMP-1/ collagenase, Tyrosinase.

Introduction

Ageing is a continuous and irresistible mechanism that takes place in all living organisms. As the age of an individual progresses, the dermal or skin ageing becomes more evident (chronological/intrinsic ageing) but excessive exposure to ultraviolet radiation also leads to ageing (premature/extrinsic ageing), if not prevented or treated.[1] Thus, the skin is the most vulnerable organ exposed to the detrimental effect of reactive oxygen species (ROS) produced as a result of its proximity with the external environment and ultraviolet radiation. These ROS produced causes the degradation of extracellular matrix (ECM) that is essential for the maintenance of structural firmness (collagen), elasticity (elastin) and hydration (hyaluronic acid) of the skin which in turn is dependent on the activity of several enzymes intricated in skin ageing like hyaluronidase, elastase, tyrosinase, and collagenase or matrix metalloproteinase-1.[2] These changes are visible as fine wrinkles, blotchiness, hyperpigmentation, dryness, etc.[3] Apart from the skin's defense mechanism against ageing, many synthetic cosmetic products like sunscreens are also available in the market but their use is limited owing to their several adverse effects like skin irritation, allergy, etc. Thus, the need for natural or herbal products is always in demand as they are more acceptable with fewer side effects. In this regard, numbers of natural compounds are evaluated for their anti-ageing potential.[4] Based on this, the present study was conducted to scientifically validate the folklore uses of *Ocimum tenuiflorum* for the protection of the skin against ageing particularly photoageing and to evaluate the leaves of the selected plant through *in- vitro* enzymatic inhibition assays.

Materials and Methods

Collection and Authentication of Plant Materials

Fresh leaves of *Ocimumtenuiflorum* L. were collected from herbal garden of the University, in month of October-November and authenticated from the Department of Botany. The voucher specimen (Reference No. VS/ Ph cog/ 2017/ 413) was submitted in the Department for future reference.

Chemicals Used

1, 1-diphenyl-2-picryl-hydrazyl (DPPH), Tris-HCL buffer, Tricine buffer, Catechin, Tris-HCL buffer, Bovine Hyaluronidase enzyme, Collagenase from *Clostridium histolyticum,* porcine pancreatic elastase, Furyl acryloyl – Leucine - Glycine Propyl Alanine (FALGPA), N - methoxysuccinyl) – ala-ala-pro-val 4-nitroanilide (MAAPVN), Albumin, Tyrosinase, Sodium hyaluronate, Acetate buffer, Dimethyl sulfoxide (DMSO), Calcium chloride, p-Dimethyl amino benzaldehyde (PDMAB) were procured from sigma Aldrich and Fluka chemicals. Other chemicals and reagents used in the present evaluation were of analytical grade.

Extraction and Fractionation of Plant Material

500gm of dried leaves of *Ocimum tenuiflorum* were taken, washed, dried and heated with water at a controlled temperature of 60° Celsius, filtered and the resultant filtrate was treated with ethyl acetate and n-butanol to get the resultant fractions. The fractions were lyophilized and kept in sealed containers for further studies.

Antioxidant studies

DPPH radical scavenging activity

The antioxidant potential of the extract was based on the inhibitory potential of the stable DPPH (1, 1-diphenyl-2picrylhydrazyl) free radical and the procedure followed was as explained by Braca et al. [5] with little changes. The extracts of *Ocimum tenuiflorum* were prepared ina dilution series (100, 200 and 300μg/ml) in Dimethyl sulfoxide

(DMSO). The reaction mixture consisted of 0.1ml test sample with 0.2ml DPPH solution (0.15 mM in 80% methanol solution). The final reaction mixture was shaken dynamically and kept at room temperature for 30 minutes in dark. Ascorbic acid was used as standard. The evaluations were done spectrophotometrically (using ELISA reader) at 517 nm and the % scavenging potential was calculated by given formula

$$\text{Inhibitory activity (\%)} = (\text{Abs}_{control} - \text{Abs}_{sample} \setminus \text{Abs}_{control}) \times 100$$

Where, Abs is the absorbance

The antioxidant potential of the extracts was demonstrated as IC_{50} (A concentration (μg/ml) which causes 50% reduction in the formation of DPPH free radicals is known as IC_{50} value of any drug or plant extract). All the observations were taken in the triplicates and graph was plotted by average.

Enzymatic studies

Hyaluronidase inhibitory activity

50μl bovine hyaluronidase (prepared by diffusing 7900 units/ml of enzyme in 0.1M acetate buffer; pH3.5) was added to 50μl of different dilutions of test extract prepared by using 5% DMSO and incubated at 37°C for 20 minutes. In the control group, 50μl of DMSO was added instead of plant extract. Hyaluronidase was activated by the addition of 50μl of calcium chloride (12.5 mM) in reaction mixture and the whole mixture was incubated for 20 minutes at 37°C. The obtained Ca^{+2}activated hyaluronidase was then treated with 250μl of sodium hyaluronate (0.1 M acetate buffer; pH3.5, was used to diffuse 1.2 mg/ml) and kept for 3 minutes on water bath at 100°C. The reaction mixture was then cooled to room temperature and added 1.5 ml of PDMAB [4 gm dissolved in glacial acetic acid (350 ml) and 10 N HCl (50 ml)]. The reaction mixture was then kept for 20 minutes at room temperature.[6] The absorbance was measured at 585nm. Inhibitory effect was calculated as:

Inhibition (%) = [(Abs $_{of\ control}$ − Abs $_{of\ sample}$) / Abs $_{of\ control}$] ×100

 Abs = Absorbance

Matrix metalloproteinase (MMP-1) / Collagenase inhibitory activity

MMP-1 / Collagenase inhibition assay was carried out on the basis of the method discussed by Kim et al.[7] It involves the use of collagenase (0.8units/ml) from *Clostridium histolyticum* and 2mM of synthetic substrate, FALGPA. The final reaction mixture contained 25µl of 50mM tricine buffer, 25µl of test sample and 25µl of collagenase enzyme (0.1 units). After the addition of 50µl of 2mM FALGPA, absorbance was immediately measured at 340 nm by ELISA reader. Catechin was used as a standard. The percentage enzyme inhibition was calculated by given formula:

Enzyme inhibition activity (%) = [1-(B/A)] ×100

Where A= activity of control, B=activity of test extracts.

Elastase inhibitory activity

Elastase inhibition activity was analyzed by the procedure discussed by Pientaweeratch et al.[8] Mix 0.1 ml of a 0.2M Tris-HCl buffer having 1% albumin, 0.025ml of 10mM MAAPVN and 0.05ml of sample of different concentrations (20µg/ml, 40µg/ml, 60µg/ml, 80 µg/ml and 100µg/ml). Then add 0.025ml of elastase (3 units /ml) to each test sample. Incubate the resultant reaction mixture at 25°C for 20 minutes and measure the absorbance by ELISA reader at 410 nm. Percentage inhibition was calculated using following formula:

Inhibition rate (%) = [1-(C-D)/ (A-B)] ×100

Where,

A and B represents the absorbance without a test sample after and before incubation respectively.

C and D represent the absorbance with a test sample after and before incubation respectively.

Tyrosinase inhibitory activity

The determination of tyrosinase was performed using L-DOPA as substrate.[9-12] Firstly, dissolve 0.8 ml of L-DOPA (2.5 mM) with 2.4 ml of phosphate buffer solution (0.067 M) of pH 6.6. Then incubate the reaction mixture for 10 minutes at 37°C. After this, 0.8 ml of 2 mg/ml extracts and 0.8 ml tyrosinase solution were mixed. The solution was instantaneously examined for generation of dopachrome by estimating linear rise in optical density for 5 minutes at 475nm. The observations were taken in triplicates. The tyrosinase inhibitory activity was estimated by the formula:

$$\text{Inhibition (\%)} = \frac{(C - D) - (A - D)}{C - D}$$

Where, A and B is absorbance of sample with L-DOPA and without L-DOPA respectively

C is the absorbance without sample and with substrate and D is the absorbance without both sample and substrate.

Statistical analysis

Results were expressed as the half maximal inhibitory concentration (IC_{50}) calculated on the basis of mean percentage inhibition $\pm$ standard deviation with readings taken thrice. Linear regression was used to analyze results for calculating the IC_{50} values.

Results

Determination of extractive value

As per procedure mentioned above for the extraction and fractionation, the yield of leaves extracts is summarized in the Table 1. These extracts were further evaluated for their antioxidant and various enzyme inhibition activities.

Table 1: Extractive value of *Ocimum tenuiflorum* leaf extracts

Sr. No	Solvent	Extractive value %W/W)
1	Ethyl acetate	1.14
2	n-butanol	1.48
3	Aqueous	8.74

Hyaluronidase inhibitory activity

The percentage of total hyaluronidase inhibitory activity and IC_{50} values of extracts of *Ocimum tenuiflorum* are presented in Table 2. The

IC_{50} value of the ethyl acetate, n-butanol and aqueous extracts of *Ocimum tenuiflorum* were found to be 65.51, 58.57 and 68.55 in comparison to that of standard catechin having the IC_{50} value 17.44 µg/ml.

Elastase inhibitory activity

The percentage of total elastase inhibitory activity and IC_{50} values of ethyl acetate, n-butanol and aqueous extracts of *Ocimum tenuiflorum* and standard are presented in Table 3. The IC_{50} value of the ethyl acetate, n-butanol and aqueous extracts of *Ocimum tenuiflorum* were found to be 66, 123 and 25.74 in comparison to that of standard catechin having the IC_{50} value 16.82 µg/ml.

Table 2: Hyaluronidase inhibitory potential of *Ocimum tenuiflorum* leaf extracts

Concentration (µg/ml)	% Inhibition (Mean ± SEM, n=3)			
	Catechin (standard)	Ethyl acetate	n-butanol	Aqueous
20	60.56±0.85	34.6±1.1	37.56±0.91	34.87±1.37
40	70.42±0.85	42.1±1.23	43.2±1.7	39.6±0.76
60	77.04±0.68	47.76±0.84	50.32±1.77	47.19±1.17

80	85.77±0.50	55.37±1.44	57.10±0.81	54.32±1.05
100	88.30±0.67	61.22±1.06	64.35±0.90	60.12±1.48
IC_{50} value(µg/ml)	17.44	65.51	58.57	68.55

Table 3: Elastase inhibitory potential of *Ocimum tenuiflorum* leaf extracts

Concentration (µg/ml)	% Inhibition (Mean ± SEM, n=3)			
	Catechin (standard)	Ethyl acetate	n-butanol	Aqueous
20	48.11±010	31.3±1.31	22.7±1.63	47.1±1.58
40	64.71±0.38	38.6±1.15	27±1.63	54.8±1.24
60	71.11±0.61	44.2±0.81	33.6±0.87	57.7±1.04
80	79.31±0.51	57.7±0.98	38.1±0.97	64.9±0.99
100	87.43±0.73	65.3±1.11	43.8±2.25	72.8±0.86
IC_{50} value(µg/ml)	16.82	66	123	25.74

MMP-1/Collagenase inhibitory activity

The percentage of total collagenase inhibitory activity and IC_{50} value of various extracts of *Ocimum tenuiflorum* and standard are presented in Table 4. The IC_{50} value of the ethyl acetate, n-butanol and aqueous extracts of *Ocimum tenuiflorum* were found to be 52.66, 42.16, 51.64 in comparison to that of standard catechin having the IC_{50} value 15.21 µg/ml.

Tyrosinase inhibitory activity

The percentage of total tyrosinase inhibitory activity and IC_{50} values of extracts of *Ocimum tenuiflorum* and standard are presented in Table 5. The IC_{50} value of the ethyl acetate, n-butanol and aqueous extracts of *Ocimum tenuiflorum* were found to be 40.06, 72.07 and 28.38 in comparison to that of standard quercetin having the IC_{50} value 17.44 µg/ml.

Table 4: MMP-1/Collagenase inhibitory potential of *Ocimum tenuiflorum* leaf extracts

Concentration (µg/ml)	% Inhibition (Mean ± SEM, n=3)			
	Catechin (standard)	Ethyl acetate	n-butanol	Aqueous
20	53.09±0.77	37.01±1.20	42.5±0.60	39.34±0.54
40	61.57±0.36	44.83±0.65	48.76±0.82	45.87±1.03
60	69.76±0.50	53.11±1.40	56.95±1.09	52.54±0.80
80	82.04±0.54	61.73±1.41	64.12±0.92	59.11±1.01
100	90.81±0.57	68.04±1.21	71.34±1.13	68.07±1.06
IC_{50} value(µg/ml)	15.21	52.66	42.16	51.64

Table 5: Tyrosinase inhibitory potential of *Ocimum tenuiflorum* leaf

extracts

Concentration (µg/ml)	% Inhibition (Mean ± SEM, n=3)			
	Quercetin (standard)	Ethyl acetate	n-butanol	Aqueous
20	64.45±2.30	57.65±0.42	34.85±1.08	61.24±1.25
40	69.01±1.52	61.02±1.71	39.26±1.40	66.26±0.76
60	75.8±1.72	72.21±1.20	46.24±1.14	71.09±1.33
80	83.87±3.51	78.02±0.27	53.28±1.08	75.56±1.31
100	91.9±2.62	82.60±0.74	58.17±0.94	80.20±0.89
IC_{50} value(µg/ml)	17.44	40.06	72.07	28.38

DPPH radical scavenging activity

The percentage inhibition and IC_{50} values of leaf extracts are presented in Table 6. The lower IC_{50} value represents the stronger antioxidant activity. Ethyl acetate extract showed activity almost half to the standard (Ascorbic acid) taken while n-butanol extract showed almost 1/3 activity to standard (Table: 6). It was observed that *Ocimum tenuiflorum* leafextracts (ethyl acetate, N-butanol and aqueous) have dose dependent DPPH radical inhibitory activity.

Table 6: Antioxidant activity of *Ocimum tenuiflorum* leaf extracts

Concentration (µg/ml)	% Inhibition (Mean ± SEM, n=3)			
	Ascorbic acid	Ethyl acetate	n-butanol extract	Aqueous extract

	(Standard)	extract		
100	62.54 ± 2.7	57.89±1.05	55.87±1.78	54.26±1.78
200	71.98 ± 2.5	67.6±1.56	64.55±1.45	63.78±2.03
300	91.3 ± 3.0	85.4±0.99	84.56±2.6	82.11±1.44
IC_{50} value(µg/ml)	24.57	52.7	72.5	80.93

Discussion

The ancient traditional system of medicine demonstrated the use of various plants, its different parts or extracts to lessen the effect of UV radiations on skin and maintain the beauty of the skin. Medicinal plants contain various phytochemical constituents which include polyphenolic compounds, alkaloids, flavonoids, tannins, carotenoids, terpinoids, etc. that exhibit potent antioxidant properties and can be used in reducing skin ageing particularly photoageing.[13] Some plants contain many other phytochemical constituents that may help in inhibition of enzyme like hyaluronidase, elastase, MMP, tyrosinase etc. which are important in controlling skin ageing.[14] In addition, these herbal products are rapidly absorbed by the skin and are hypoallergic in nature making them more acceptable in the society.

Hyaluronic acid, a glycosaminoglycan, consists of D-glucuronic acid and N-acetyl-D-glucosamine units linked by a glucuronidic β $(1{\rightarrow}3)$ bond.[15] It helps to bind and retain water molecules in the skin thus keeping the body smooth, moist and lubricated. The reduction in the hyaluronic acid levels along with breakdown of collagen and elastin lead to changes associated with aged skin like sagging, wrinkle formation, decreased elasticity and reduced efficiency to assist the microvasculature of the skin.[16] The n-butanol extract showed highest hyaluronidase inhibiton in comparison to other extracts and showed 30% inhibition in comparison to standard (Catechin) at IC_{50} value (Table: 2).

Elastase, a proteolytic enzyme that hydrolyses the peptide bond of elastin, breaks down elastin and elastic fibers which along with collagen provides structural framework and elasticity to the skin. This brings about the change in the mechanical characteristics of connective tissue and is directly connected with skin photoageing. Loss of elasticity of skin by elastases leads to sagging.[16] Aqueous extract showed highest elastase inhibitory activity in comparison to other extracts at all tested concentrations and inhibited elastase by 82% and 64% in comparison to standard (Catechin) at concentration 100 µg/ml and IC_{50} value respectively (Table: 3).

MMPs are mainly seven types and are a group of zinc-containing extracellular proteinases.[17] Mainly, MMP-1/collagenase is enzyme that breaks the peptide bonds in collagen which is responsible for giving strength and firmness to skin. Collagenase is produced by two separate and distinct genes in *Clostridium histolyticum* and is inhibited by α_2 - macroglobulin, a large plasma glycoprotein.[18] The n-butanol extract showed highest Collagenase inhibiton (71%) among other extracts at concentration 100 µg/ml and the positive control, Catechin, inhibited the collagenase activity 91% at same concentration. The n-butanol extract showed 36% inhibition in comparison to standard (Catechin) at IC_{50} value (Table: 4).

Tyrosinase is a copper containing enzyme that catalyzes the rate -
limiting steps in the production of melanin (an important pigment that
helps to protect the skin from UV damage) i.e. hydroxylation of L-
tyrosine to the 3, 4-dihydroxyphenylalanine (DOPA) and the oxidation
of DOPA to dopaquinone.[19] Melanin also acts as a vital defense
system of skin against other harmful factors.[20] Hence, inhibiting the
tyrosinase enzyme shows skin whitening effect or anti-hyperpigment
agent as it represses the production of melanin. The aqueous extract
showed highest anti-tyrosinase activity in comparison to other extracts
and showed 61% tyrosinase inhibition in comparison to standard
(Quercetin) at IC_{50} value (Table: 5).

According to the knowledge of authors, this plant has not yet been
screened for anti-ageing potential. However, plants of other species,
belonging to the same genus and family have been studied for this
activity.[21] In the present study, the antioxidant, MMP-1/collagenases,
hyaluronidase, tyrosinase and elastase inhibitory activity of various
extracts of *Ocimum tenuiflorum* were determined using ELISA reader.
The polyphenolic compounds are mainly responsible for the
antioxidant potential of plant extracts.[21] The essential oil from arial
parts of *Ocimum   tenuiflorum* has been found to contain methyl
eugenol, β-caryophyllene, borneol, germacrene D, α-pinene, and α-
copaene.[22] It is believed that the presence of these polyphenolic
compounds along with some other potential phytochemicals may have
contributed to the protective role against skin ageing enzymes which is
demonstrated in the present study. Such potential and promising
therapeutic activity of this plant showed its use in folklore medicine.

Further studies can be carried out to find out the exact mechanisms behind the observed activity.

Conclusion

Thus, *Ocimum tenuiflorum* leaf extracts showed significant anti-hyaluronidase, anti-collagenase, antielastase and anti-tyrosinase activities which may prove as important ingredient in cosmetic industrial products meant for ageing skin.

References

1. Jadoon S, Karim S, Bin Asad MHH, Akram MR, Khan AK, Arif Malik A, et al. Anti-ageing potential of phytoextract loaded-pharmaceutical creams for human skin cell longetivity. Oxidative Medicine and Cellular Longevity 2015;2015:1-17

2. Ndlovu G, Fouche G, Tselanyane M, Cordier W, Steenkamp V. *In vitro* determination of the anti-ageing potential of four southern African medicinal plants. BMC Complement Alter Med 2013;13:304.

3. Duraivel S, Shaheda SA, Basha SR, Pasha SE, Jilani S. Formulation and evaluation of Antiwrinkle activity of Cream and Nano emulsion of Moringa oleifera seed oil. IOSR-PBS 2014;9:58-73.

4. Fang EF, Scheibye-Knudsen M, Vilhelm A, Bohr, Ng TB. The Anti-Ageing Efficacy of Natural Compounds. Med Aromat Plants 2012;1-2.

5. Braca A, Tommasi ND, Bari LD, Pizza C, Politi M, Morelli I. Antioxidant principles from *Bauhinia terapotensis*. J Nat Prod 2001;64:892-5.

6. Lee BC, Lee SY, Lee HJ, Sim GS, Kim JH, Kim J. Antioxidative and photo protective effects of coumarins isolated from *Fraxinus chinensis*. Arch Dermatol Res 2007;30:1293-301.

7. Kim YJ, Uyama H, Kobayashi S. Inhibition effects of (+)-catechin-aldehyde polycondensates on proteinases causing proteolytic degradation of extracellular matrix. Biochem Biophys Res Comm 2004;320:256-61.

8. Pientaweeratch S, Panapisa V, Tansirikongkol Y. Antioxidant, anti-collagenase and anti-elastase activities of *Phyllanthus emblica, Manilkara zapota* and silymarin: an *in vitro* comparative study for anti-ageing applications. Pharm Biol 2016;54:1865-72.

9. Hsu C, Chang C, Lu H, Chung Y. Inhibitory effects of the water extracts of Lavendula sp. on mushroom tyrosinase activity. Food Chem 2007;105:1099-105.

10. Wang BS, Chang LW, Wu HC, Huang SL, Chu HL, Huang MH. Antioxidant and antityrosinase activity of aqueous extracts of green asparagus. Food Chem 2011;127:141-6.

11. Jiménez M, Chazarra S, Escribano J, Cabanes J, García-Carmona F. Competitive inhibition of mushroom tyrosinase by 4-substituted benzaldehydes. J Agric Food Chem 2001;49:4060-3.

12. Kubo I, Kinst-Hori I. Tyrosinase inhibitory activity of the olive oil flavor compound. J Agric Food Chem 1999;47:4574-8.

13. Cavinato M, Waltenberger B, Baraldo G, Grade CVC, Stuppner H, Jansen-Dürr P. Plant extracts and natural compounds used against UVB-induced photoageing. Biogerontology 2017;18:499–516.

14. Liyanaarachchi GD, Samarasekera JKRR, Mahanama R, Hemalal P. Tyrosinase, elastase, hyaluronidase, inhibitory and antioxidant activity of Sri Lankan medicinal plants for novel cosmeceuticals. Industrial Crops and Products. 2018;111:597-605.

15. Papakonstantinou E, Roth M, and Karakiulakis G. Hyaluronic acid: A key molecule in skin ageing. Dermato endocrinol 2012;4:253–58.

16. Imokawa G, Ishida K. Biological Mechanisms Underlying the Ultraviolet Radiation-Induced Formation of Skin Wrinkling and Sagging I: Reduced Skin Elasticity, Highly Associated with Enhanced Dermal Elastase Activity, Triggers Wrinkling and Sagging. Int. J Mol Sci 2015;16:7753-75.

17. Millis AJT, Hoyle M, McCue HM, Martini H. Differential expression of metalloproteinase and tissue inhibitor of metalloproteinase genes in aged human fibroblasts. Experimental Cell Research 1992;201:373–79.

18. Yoshihara K, Matsushita O, Minami J, Okabe A. Cloning and nucleotide sequence analysis of the *colH* gene from *Clostridium histolyticum* encoding a collagenase and a gelatinase. J Bacteriol. 1994;176:6489–96.

19. Tiwari, P, Kumar B, Kaur M, Kaur G, Kaur H. Phytochemical screening and extraction: A review. Internationale Pharmaceutica Sciencia. 2011;1:98-106.

20. Petrillo AD, González-Paramás AM, Era B, Medda R, Pintus F, Santos-Buelga C, et al. Tyrosinase inhibition and antioxidant properties of Asphodelus microcarpus extracts. BMC Complementary and Alternative Medicine 2016;16:453.

21. Hakkim FL, Arivazhagan G, Boopathy R. Antioxidant property of selected *Ocimum* species and their secondary metabolite content. Journal of Medicinal Plants Research. 2008;2:250-7.

22. Joshi RK, Hoti S. Chemical composition of the essential oil of *Ocimum tenuiflorum* L. (Krishna Tulsi) from North West Karnataka, India. Plant Science Today. 2014;1:99-102.

Thanks for reading this book.

For more information about medicinal plants having anti-ageing and anti-wrinkle potential, their actions, traditional methods and proven home remedies to control skin related problems, please feel free to contact:

Chanchal Garg, PhD
Post Doctoral Research Fellow (UGC-PDFW)
Department of Pharmaceutical Sciences,
Maharshi Dayanand University,
Rohtak, haryana, India
cgarg72@gmail.com